INVESTING FOR TEENS

7-Step System of Beginner's Stock Market Secrets for Teenagers to Achieve Financial Freedom by Age 21

JP Clarke

$149 FREE BONUS

jp-clarke.com

CONTENTS

Want to receive all my future books for FREE before they are released to the public?

Visit jp-clarke.com/reviewteam to find out more.

$149

FREE

INVESTMENT
RESOURCES

INVESTING CHEATSHEET

TOP 3 STOCKS TO BUY NOW

110 PASSIVE INCOME IDEAS

COMPANY RESEARCH STRATEGY

Download Now

jp-clarke.com/bonus

INTRODUCTION

LEARN TO INVEST IN STOCKS

"We don't need to be smarter than the rest; we have to be more disciplined than the rest"
— **Warren Buffet**

Will you believe me if I tell you that you can earn $78,000 as a teen in just a few short months? Most probably not! Christon "The Truth" Jones, a 14-year-old student-athlete from Mississippi, often bullied by his peers, spent much of his free time trading stocks. Christon got his passion for trading stocks when he heard about another 14-year-old teen from Chicago who made $50,000 in the stock market after having bought stocks in Nike when his mom refused to allow him to buy a pair of trainers before he owned some shares in the company. Christon was instantly inspired by this story and started learning about the stock market. His passion paid off big time when he made his first $10,000 in his early trades, which included Amazon shares, using his mom's trading account. In March 2020, the stock market took a hit as the COVID-19 pandemic struck. When most investors went into panic mode as prices fell, Christon snatched up shares in Tesla, the famous electric-car company. These were trading at around $72 per share but were soon up to $300 by July. When he and his mom eventually decided to sell, they made $78,000 off a single trade in only a few months! The Tesla stock later reached an all-time high of $900 in January 2021. According to a study by Deutsche Bank, a new wave of successful teen traders has emerged during the pandemic.

Christon "The Truth" Jones is now an acclaimed investor and entrepreneur, featuring in many international headlines and speaking at seminars, teaching kids to become successful. Christon's take on investing is, *"It's much more fun to buy stuff when you know you own part of the company, so I like to splurge on X-Box games, and of course, Amazon is my first choice when my mom has to order stuff."* No longer does he have to worry about paying his college fees or whether his mom will be able to make ends meet. He doesn't need to second-guess spending an extra $50 on a nice meal with his friends or buying the latest Nike Air Jordans. His future is carved with excellence, and many thrilling endeavors await him. He can ensure his family has the life they always dreamed of. Attracting wealth at a young age through stocks is one thing, but gaining the mindset of an investor and an entrepreneur is another. Christon learned to harness both at a very young age.

While there are kids who spend their lunch breaks and free time on mundane activities such as gossiping, pulling pranks, and getting up to no good, some kids are making millions! Your success is only a decision away; which decision will you make? To be successful, or not? A tiny bit of discipline to avoid the distraction, coupled with the knowledge of how the stock market works, could transform your future into the all-American dream! Don't wait! It's your turn now! How would you feel if you had already achieved your goals and accomplished financial independence by the age of 21? How would you feel if you could afford to buy whatever you dreamed of without even thinking about it? For most people, achieving success in this area is not an easy task. Christon discovered the same rules and principles outlined in this book to attain his ultimate dream—now, you shall have it too.

Let me offer you a glimpse of what you will benefit from the upcoming chapters:

- A simplified 7-step guide to help you get started in the world of stocks.

- A strategic plan enabling you to start investing and become financially independent by the time you turn 21.

- A complete knowledge of the stock market, its working, principles, and laws.

- The ins and outs of how to buy and sell stocks.

- The understanding of necessary tools and how to use them during the journey of becoming an investor.

- The wisdom of an experienced mentor who will guide you through each step, ensuring your victory.

- Understanding and mastering the skills required to succeed.

And a lot more...

If you're a parent, then it is settled that nobody can love your child more than you do. Besides loving them unconditionally and fulfilling all their desires, you also have a more important duty on your hands, i.e., ensuring that your kids are financially independent. I enthuse you to make use of this book to teach your precious child the art of saving money and investing in building a fortune in the coming future. Children grow up quickly, and the world does not show mercy on anyone. Therefore, you must prepare them for the upcoming life struggles. This book can teach beginners of all ages, not only teens. It can help you learn everything about the stock market, from the stock's fundamentals to even the more traditional buying and selling strategies. In addition to your day job, you too can start investing in stocks and become a role model who fulfills your child's curious mind, enabling them to indulge in the mastery of investments.

The goal is to get them started as young as possible to be settled in their finances when they approach their teens and early adulthood. But unfortunately, most people get involved in various attractive-looking investments which turn out to be fads. They lose all their money as they have no idea about the inner workings and processes.

If you're a teen who's reading this, then be reassured that most teenagers like you have the potential to build an empire for themselves; the only missing link is the correct guidance. This book will become a catalyst that drives you towards the dream you foresee for yourself and future generations. Are you looking to invest your money? Well, let me introduce you to the realm of stocks.

I know what you may be thinking—stocks aren't easy money; it probably takes a lot of time and effort. Only a professional stock investor could make a fortune out of it, not any random kid. But perhaps, this book will change your perspective. Peter Lynch said, *"Everybody has the power to follow the stock market. If you made it through fifth-grade math, you can do it."*

Moreover, investing in stocks is one of the best ways to make a providence of profit. All you need is the proper direction and determination. Armed with these weapons in your arsenal, this book could change the trajectory of your life forever.

To get started, there is no doubt you will need to master the art of earning and saving money. All you must do is budget for what you need to comfortably survive daily, then set the rest aside to compound your investments. We all know what it means to save money. I won't insult your intelligence explaining to you its definition, but one thing we need is discipline. Discipline in realizing the short-term sacrifices we need to make to achieve our long-term ambitions. The only question is, how much do you want it? Whether delivering pizzas or making multi-million-dollar trades on the stock market, the principle remains unchanged. Sacrifice a little now so that tomorrow, you can prosper! It is all too easy to be persuaded by the bright, shiny attraction of the latest, coolest gear or going out all the time with your friends. It doesn't take long for your money to dissipate gracefully, especially with the constant anxiety of having to keep up with peer pressure. The mere fact that you selected this book signifies that you are indeed planning a bright future for yourself to become financially independent. Perhaps you want to make a better life for yourself, your parents, and your family, or you are a caring parent who wishes to see your child succeed in the real world. This easy 7-step system will guide you through a complete investment strategy, taking you from a beginner to your first successful trade.

You do not have to feel nervous and be scared that you're young and nobody will take your commitments seriously enough. It's okay if you don't understand anything about the stock market, or you feel lost with loads of questions in your head about investing. Don't let this intimidate you into believing that the stock market is only for adults. You, too, could make a difference using this classic method of earning a fantastic income. Your dream will be realized once you apply the lessons you learn ahead. This could also be the point where you no longer need to live off your parents' money—as you will be making your own.

Now, you may be questioning who I am and how I gained the expertise regarding this particular subject of stock investment? So, let me tell you a bit about myself and the purpose behind writing this book. My name is J.P. Clarke, an experienced author, investor, and serial entrepreneur. I started my very first business at only eight years old. I, like you, started investing from a young age, so I know the struggles you will face. I later got into real estate, building a multi-million-dollar portfolio, and I've been studying the stock market, its strategies, and its potential for years. My love for the stock market inspired me to conduct countless research and trial-runs buying and selling. With hard work, perseverance, and some sacrifice, I achieved financial freedom at a very young age. After investing most of my time into understanding stocks, I witnessed patterns about what needed to be done to become successful. What you're about to learn is adopted by many teenagers. You can also comprehend the same insights to make your own money and lead a financially comfortable life. This book is the result of rigorous trial and error in my personal investment experience that will teach you and many teenagers like you the art of becoming a stock investor.

My mission is to resolve your pains and guide you through the world of stocks, so you too, could steer in the driving seat and be in control of your life. American entrepreneur Mark Cuban once said, *"If you don't follow the stock market, you are missing some amazing drama."* A great investor is the result of discipline and good habits. Building successful habits is a crucial component. The habits of discipline, investing before you blow your money, earning, allocating a specific amount of money periodically to invest in a particular stock, and many more. Writer Will Durant said, *"We are what we repeatedly do. Excellence, then, is not an act but a habit."*

This book will teach you the importance of the stock market and why you should explore its territory and start investing right now. The road to stocks may not be easy, but learning the key terms and specifics will go a long way.

Moreover, you will comprehend how to get started in the game of stocks by understanding what to do and what not to do. I will make sure that you know all the stock market basics and what it actually is. You will come across multiple techniques and methods that will help you decide what to invest in and which stocks to pick. Keeping track of all the profitable stocks could get a little complicated. Having an organized setup is also a key ingredient in building appropriate strategies and making you successful. Let me warn you that you will face some serious pitfalls and obstacles in your journey. They are inevitable, but you could glide past them if you're prepared for them beforehand. Further in the book, you will learn to dodge the mistakes and prevail. This will help you learn from your own experience as an investor, which you will rely upon in your future strategies to make intelligent decisions.

American investor and philanthropist Peter Lynch once mentioned that *"the real key to making money in stocks is to not get scared out of them."* You might feel a slight resistance within yourself, but push past that setback, and you will be on a fast track towards gaining your financial confidence.

Now, it's time to take you on the journey towards meeting your financial dream. First, let's begin with a deeper understanding of the stock market and why you should choose it as your investment solution—prepare yourself to walk on the *"road to stocks."*

CHAPTER 1

THE ROAD TO STOCKS

"An important key to investing is to remember that stocks are not lottery tickets."

– Peter Lynch

A re you looking for the highest potential investment returns? Your research brought you right into it. There are thousands of investment options out there, and since the beginning, stocks have been the go-to investment strategy for most investors. Your investment portfolio is incomplete without it. You'll notice if you look attentively that, over the long term, no other type of investment performs better. Hence, it provides a sense of relief that you will meet all your future goals once compounding takes effect. I can't adequately emphasize how crucial it is to own stocks as an investor. It will help you to accumulate wealth and enjoy the fruits of your labor. Studying how the stock market works or teaching your kids the same will set them up for life. In this chapter, you will grasp the importance of the stock market and why you should invest your time and money into it.

You may have friends or relatives who invest their money in the latest technology or some unreal cryptocurrencies or other investments that don't make much sense to you. Still, in reality, you must invest only in the things you understand in order to be successful in those investments. Do not fall victim to peer pressure. I strive to teach you about the ins and outs of the stock market and give you a forged plan of execution to sustain your financial independence. As a teenager, your needs are met by your parents, but you want to live an independent life, don't you? For that, you must know how the world works and understand a term called *inflation*.

It is the increase in the price of goods and services that you commonly use, over time. But how does that affect us, you ask? Well, due to inflation, the value of the dollar goes down each year, which is also referred to as its purchasing power. It doesn't sound that great of a deal, but trust me, it is. Because with the $100 you have in your bank today, you will not be able to buy the same amount of stuff in, say, three years. Let's look at people with a stable income with no annual pay rise; their daily essentials cost more each year as things become more expensive over time. Yet, their salaries aren't increasing and therefore, eventually, isn't enough to handle the burden.

Why am I telling you this? Because your hard-earned money is simply decreasing by sitting idle in your bank account. You worked hard for months to earn the money you have, most likely at a low-paid unfulfilling job like most other teens. Would you be happy knowing that it is losing value every day? Of course not! Fortunately for you, there is a simple way out. All you need is to ensure that the return you earn from any investment is higher than the annual inflation rate. Who decides the inflation rate? It is determined by the markets and is dependent on certain economic factors. Each country has its own inflation rate and is usually decided by that country's central bank. In the US, the Federal Reserve will set policies that alter inflation. At the end of 2020, the US inflation rate was 1.25%.

Stocks defy the effect of inflation, and when you hold a stock for a long time, you are building yourself a fortune as it will likely increase in value over the long run. Does investing in stocks sound complex to you? Don't worry; it is actually a flexible and straightforward approach to the wealth creation process. All you need is a productive mindset, accurate knowledge, the proper guidance, and a habit of discipline. That's it. Wait! You also need a trading account and a DEMAT account, which we will get into later, but that's it. After that, you're all set to go!

WHY INVEST IN STOCKS NOW?

You can start investing any time. So, why am I encouraging you to invest in your teenage years? Aren't your teenage years meant for fun, parties, making friends, and enjoying a carefree life? Perhaps it is. But how cool do you think it would be when you realize that most people you're hanging out with today still struggle financially later in their lives because they didn't plan for success early on and end up living a life of misery? Not very cool at all! That is why I want you to be successful early on in life, ensuring your finances are in order, and you can worry less about your future. And don't stress, investing early doesn't mean you won't have any fun. You will have loads of time for fun, and just think how cool it will be when you can afford to throw the best parties ever! Not to mention being able to buy all the clothes, gadgets, and accessories you could ever dream of, being the envy of all your friends!

Isn't that how it should be? Come on; I want to hear it from you, what will you choose? Ten years of fun and sixty years of misery? Or five to ten years of discipline and lifelong freedom? Anyone with a rational mind will choose the latter, but we don't find it familiar for some reason. Instead, we see kids fooling around, pulling pranks, participating in meaningless activities, and wasting their precious time and energy. I am not saying you cannot do that; you can do that as well if you want, provided there is an assurance.

I'm not attempting to put a damper on the party. I am trying to tell you that learning how to invest right now when you're still a teenager can set you up financially for your future and allow you to have all the fun in the world then. In a sense, it will start you on the road to complete financial independence. *Money is the most powerful tool in the whole world.* Whatever anyone says, I don't care; it is true! Anybody without it struggles. You will not be one of them. The mere fact that you have acquired this book means that you are different from others and want to make your life count. I appreciate your determination and your decisions.

Your parents may not realize this, but kids these days are more capable and developed than ever. You have a curious and creative mind. You're sharp, and you learn fast. Furthermore, you don't have any negative emotions like fear of failure stopping you from applying the knowledge you learn and possess. You have the exact combination for success. Learn from this book and surprise your friends and family with how much you know about the stock market and investment. It all comes down to proper education and guidance. This easy guide will surely grant you in-depth knowledge about how you can invest a small portion of your money now and receive an exponential profit in the future.

There is another reason I am inspiring you to invest early. Because you will have the time to bounce back over your errors. Nobody is perfect, and everybody is prone to making mistakes. I certainly made many of them, but there is nothing to be ashamed of; it's all part of the learning experience. When you are young and have the most significant asset by your side—time, the world is your oyster! You are free to make as many blunders as you can and learn from them, gain wisdom, and don't repeat them. It will form another layer of experience referring to your personal life. You will understand the things that are to be avoided and thereby learn to do the right thing from the outset, making an even bigger profit in the future. It is as Thomas Edison, one of the greatest inventors of all time, said, *"I've not failed. I've just found 10,000 ways that won't work."*

If you're 50 years old, you don't have the same privilege of having time for making errors. You cannot afford to go wrong with your investment options and strategies; thus, you will take fewer risks and play it safe to survive. This usually means taking lower profits. With higher risk comes the potential for higher reward, and vice versa. Starting young means you can afford to take more calculated risks, and in turn, make higher profits.

THE LONG-TERM OPPORTUNITIES

Investing in stocks is like embellishing your own future. In a way, it is a vault of money used for emergencies or to live a comfortable existence in the later phase of life. So, when you're retired and wish to live a lazy and fulfilled life around your loved ones, without worrying about money—this investment will come in handy. And by the way, retirement doesn't have to be when you're old and gray! Starting early could mean retiring in your 30s or even 20s if you are highly successful and start early enough. The stock market has made many young millionaires.

Investing in the stock market not only provides you with additional savings but also teaches you the big difference between short-term and long-term thinking. The money you don't need right now could be utilized to fund a better tomorrow. American engineer, Charles Noble, said, *"You must have long-term goals to keep you from being frustrated by short-term failures."* It is important to notice that when you invest regularly, it builds a powerful habit that will help you throughout your life. Tons of people make thousands every day on the stock market. Getting into the game now and growing a habit out of it can help you become one of those incredible beings. One of the most critical skills that will help you manage your finances is investing your money.

As a teen, you have an unfair advantage of time. You probably have more years for compounding to showcase its magic. Investing a little bit now and a small definite portion every month can quickly turn into a fortune of wealth in only a few years. You will be astonished to see the results. For instance, 10% annual returns could double your investment in about seven years. Invest $500; it will turn into $1000, and so on.

Ashu Sehrawat is a top stock trader and one of the youngest self-made millionaires in India. At age 22, he became an inspiration to millions. Being exposed to entrepreneurship at the young age of 18, he quickly gained interest in the stock market. Being the son of a successful businessman, he noticed that his father reinvested all his small business profits into stocks and made a lot of money from it. Seeing how hard his father worked on his businesses, the required labor, and the hours it took out of him, this idea of creating more money out of nothing but a laptop and an internet connection was enough to get him hooked. So, he began researching the stock market, its workings, strategies, and so much more. He then opened a trading account and started his journey towards financial freedom.

He went through many failures and losses. That's when he took the time to watch and learn from traders like Derrick, Eric, and Phil. He learned short selling tactics for some time and placed his first trade. He made a profit and indulged himself in buying and selling stocks. He realized there are two key components for maximizing profits as a short-term trader—patience and selectiveness. If you keep your head calm and select stocks wisely, you will be amazed by the results. He has demonstrated to the world that you can be successful regardless of your background, upbringing, or environment.

DEMYSTIFYING THE MYTHS

As with everything in the world, people have conjured up myths about the stock market. It is one of the primary reasons people are scared of investing in the first place. They believe every imaginary assumption they hear from their peers, colleagues, and relatives who are only involved in stocks as a hobby or have an opinion yet have never bought a stock in their lives. Then, without any confirmation or proper education, they pass on the same misguided information to others. This could hurt your judgment and eventually build up negative thoughts within your own mind. That's why I will debunk some of the most common myths about the stock market to protect you from future harm and discouragement. Here are some of the typical myths you will hear:

1. Your money is safe with an Investing Virtuoso

Some people don't have the required time to learn about stocks as they are too busy in their businesses, jobs, or daily lives. Hence, they seek help from a pro-investor who manages multiple accounts all at once. These investment managers promise victory at every stage. But there is no guarantee that their strategies will always make you a profit. Some virtuosos are experts at what they do. In contrast, others may only get their reputations from luck or support rather than individual accomplishment.

Well, the same goes for you as well. Not everybody can make clear judgments leading to profits. Still, there is a myth that once you hire a pro, you don't have to worry about failures anymore. This assertion must be demystified. Indeed, there are a select few players who score every time, but what are the chances of you working with one of them? Slim! Let's be honest; nobody is more concerned about your life than yourself. Your investment manager won't go the extra mile for you. They will not take additional risks to ensure profit for you; their only concern is that they get paid well. Only you are capable of such marvels. It's better if you take charge and spend some time learning so that you can make decisions on your own behalf and not rest your fate in the hands of some stranger to make you rich when their primary goal is simply to enrich themselves.

2. Famous stocks are always safe to buy

Another myth that could blind your judgment is buying the stocks of a famous company. It is true that well-known companies are attractive for investors but do not fall victim to such a mentality. Current glory does not secure the future's position. Stocks like Apple, Vanguard, Verizon, Walmart, and more, may seem a viable option because of their track record, and they may well be. Still, many similar companies like Kodak and General Electric collapsed, resulting in losses for everyone involved. To assume that all famous companies will make you rich is a myth and one that must be demystified. Do your own research and plan for success, as well as failures.

3. You should buy what's trending in the news

This is another myth that traps many investors within its clutches. People mostly have a herd mentality; they will notice some temporary success through the news or friends and believe it will be permanent. They are following in the paths of their friends or what they've seen in the news, eventually meeting definite loss in the process. What's currently trending wasn't so popular in the past and may not be viable for all investors in the future. Do not make decisions entirely on the basis of the news you hear. Look at the company's history; what does it stand for? Are they passionate? Is there a demand? Are people buying from them? Is there a future scope for the product or services they sell? Ask many such questions, then assess their financials. This will eliminate multiple options right out the window and leave you with a select few that are much more likely to turn profitable.

4. Fast-growing companies are an excellent investment

Again, not entirely valid. Just because a company is growing rapidly NOW doesn't mean that the same will happen in the future or become stable. You must be prepared for uncertainty in the stock market, and being overly optimistic may become a losing strategy. While it may be growing rapidly now, in the following years, the craze could disappear, and the company may end up stagnant. However, it is not supposed to be your doom, and that's why you should be cautious. Do not miss the opportunity, though. You may still invest a small portion in testing the waters, but do not be overly indulged. Even if you see some great returns initially, take some time and monitor it before going all in. Again, research is essential in determining the company's future potential.

5. Follow your gut always

It is excellent advice, but unfortunately, it is not applicable when it comes to stocks. Stock market investing depends on your analytical skills. Do not try to win ground by just your instincts alone. It might betray you. Even if your gut is urging you to go ahead with an investment, and you've read dozens of quotes online like, *"Always follow your gut, it knows what your head hasn't figured out yet,"* do not rush yourself. Take a step back, breathe, analyze, and forge a strategy. Your victory will only be assured if your gut works in harmony with your analytical thesis. Research is the basis for your decision, not your gut feelings.

6. Investing in stock will take too much time

It is true that those who buy and hold are probably in it for years, if not decades, but that doesn't mean that you too must wait for that long to see any profits. It also doesn't mean that you should be a day trader hooked up on CNBC 24 hours a day for constant incline and decline so you can sell and buy proportionately. It is a myth that the stock market will consume all your time. Some investors commit part-time and still make a decent return out of it. It will take a little bit of time, especially when you're only starting out. You might spend 10+ hours researching, but you can strategically make decisions and save time in the process once you've mastered it.

7. Only rich people can invest in stocks

Clearly untrue. You can buy stocks for under $1! To invest in the stock market, you definitely don't' have to be rich. There are thousands of people who started with nothing yet made a fortune. More money could indeed provide you with more profit, but that is only when the investment is well researched and analyzed. There are stocks for everybody. Of course, some are expensive, but you can stay away from them initially and invest only in an inexpensive stock and work your way up towards the more attractive ones. Do not get discouraged and eliminate the stock market only because of a myth that forces you to do so. Invest only what you can afford, reinvest the profits and keep building on it.

8. The stock market is complex for average investors

As I mentioned before, it is not complex at all. Ordinary people see professionals perform complex calculations and formulate burdensome strategies to profit. Hence, they believe it is only for intelligent individuals, but that is certainly not the case. Buying low and selling high is all there is to it. Anyone with a bit of knowledge of basic math can possess the brainpower to invest in stocks. Never think that you're not good enough; it's an unhealthy habit that will confine you over the years and never let you exceed your limits. Instead, firmly believe that anything is possible if you add a little work and dedication behind it.

9. It's impossible to beat the market

I already told you, nothing is impossible. Many stock market millionaires will agree with me. People draw lines at various places, constraining themselves to it. Yes, it is difficult to beat the market and gain exponential profits. Still, nobody said it's impossible because people have been doing it for years. Many strategies could enable you to beat the market; you need patience and a lot of research to attain it—but you can do it. With discipline and analysis, you will witness that some well-executed strategies hold the capabilities to beat the market. Do not let the myth convince you otherwise.

10. Stocks are similar to gambling

A well-planned myth from people with little knowledge or who are lazy and do not understand the stock market, instead choosing to criticize the method. They are fearful of it, do not want to learn, and have very little knowledge of the workings of the markets. Due to this circumstance, they acknowledge the stock market as dangerous and unpredictable and brand it as gambling. While in reality, it is not. It is not a game of probability that could turn either way. On the contrary, many proven strategies could make you an extensive amount of profit over the long term, based on technical analysis rather than on a wing and a prayer.

The list was long, but it was necessary to debunk the myths before getting you started so that nothing is holding you back. So, now that nothing is clouding your mind from moving forward, let's step on the gas and roll on to the next chapter, where you will learn to speak the language of the stock market. It's the first step within the 7-step process, but before we wind up here, let us review what we learned in this chapter to make sure we are on the same page.

SUMMARY

1. Stocks are the most important options in your investment portfolio. Over the long term, no other type of investment performs better. It provides a sense of relief that you will meet all your future goals once compounding takes effect.

2. Do not fall victim to peer pressure. Instead, invest only in the things you understand.

3. Inflation is the increase in the price of goods and services that you commonly use. Stocks defy the effect of inflation and taxes because you are creating a return (profit) that is higher than inflation, essentially beating inflation. And when you hold a stock for a long time, you are building yourself a fortune.

4. Stocks are a simple and flexible approach to the wealth creation process.

5. You should invest in stocks right now because the earlier you get in, the more it will benefit you in the long run. Also, time is with you to help you bounce back from your errors.

6. Kids nowadays can achieve anything. Nothing is stopping them.

7. The stock market is riddled with misconceptions putting people off. Do not fall victim to them.

CHAPTER 2

STEP 1

SPEAK THE LANGUAGE OF STOCKS

"The stock market is filled with individuals who know the price of everything, but the value of nothing."

– Philip Fisher

C an two people have a very deep and meaningful connection without understanding the language they each speak? I don't think so! The same idea holds true for the relationship between you and the stock market. If you wish to thrive in this world, you better understand the language necessary to advance forward. This chapter will make you familiar with specific terms that you will come across during your investment career. It will help you to rectify the language and gain the upper hand when an opportunity presents itself. You don't need to be anxious about learning a whole new foreign language; it is pretty easy. You only need to be aware of a few terms that you will likely encounter in your stock market investment journey.

The language could be intimidating for beginners, as there are many things to comprehend. One simple solution is to learn the basic terms so that you will know exactly what they are talking about the next time you watch any financial news. Furthermore, I don't have to tell you about the treatment one receives when perceived as speaking professionally, do I? That person is taken as an expert and an authority in the field. Incorporating these terms into your vocabulary will make you sound like a pro.

There is no need to be left out of a conversation only because the words discussed are new to your ears. This chapter is the first step in the 7-step system designed to set you in the right direction towards a career as a professional investor. First, I will brief you about each term and then explain the meaning, where it can be used, and more. As Robert Arnott mentioned, *"In investing, what is comfortable, is rarely profitable."* So, stray beyond your comfort zone, and let's learn a new language to transform your outcome tremendously.

WHY LEARN THE NEW LANGUAGE?

This question might have occurred to you since the beginning of the chapter; let me answer it for you. Well, look at it this way, why not? The stock market is a giant world filled with both professionals and amateurs. You will be going up against some big players in the stock market who have played the game for quite some time. They have tasted the sweetness of victory and the sours of defeat during their individual journeys. They have made themselves capable of so much through their experiences. During their quest, they eventually become familiar with the language of stocks. They speak it regularly as they immerse themselves in the stock market and become experts in their fields.

If you wish to keep up with them and understand what they are talking about, you need to learn and speak the same language. When you start investing, you will come across several words and terms that will make you scratch your head and roll your eyes. So many people get scared the minute they read some bulky terms of agreement and don't understand it. Thus, they choose not to go ahead with the investment. You don't have to be that person who misses an opportunity simply because the agreement spills words that don't exist in your everyday vocabulary, leading you not to understand.

This fact will forever be changed after you finish acknowledging this chapter. When you understand the materials you're reading and what you're getting yourself into, you can be far more comfortable and assured while investing your money in the stock market. Finally, you seem ready and convinced to speak the language of stocks; so, let me take you right into it.

LEARNING THE TERMINOLOGIES

The following are some common terms people in the stock market world use. Learn them thoroughly, and you will speak the language fluently.

- **Buy**: It means to buy shares or take a position in a company. This is the whole reason you joined the stock market in the first place to *buy* the stocks you feel are profitable after doing thorough research. You can then hold the purchased stocks for an extended period of time and wait for the company to become successful, or you can sell them.

- **Sell**: It means selling or getting rid of the stocks you purchased that you currently hold. There are just two methods in which the stocks you own could make you some money. First, you buy shares, and then the resultant company increases its net worth, bringing profit to you and every other shareholder as dividends. Or second, you can sell the stocks when you see that their price has increased since you first bought them. The distinction between your purchase price and selling price is your profit.

- **Bid**: It is the amount you are willing to pay for a stock. It is important to know because this is where things get fascinating. When another trader offers to sell their stocks, you get to bid an amount you are willing to buy them. When the price drops to that determined range or precisely to that amount you bid, you can then go ahead and buy the stocks from them. Therefore, think of it as a negotiation; your bid is the price you are offering to pay.

- **Ask**: When traders want to sell their stocks, they describe a specific price for the buyers; this amount is called the asking price. It is essentially the price they are looking to achieve for their stocks.

- **Bid-Ask-Spread**: During a trade, the seller will be bidding a selling price, and the buyer will get to bid a buying price. The gap between the highest price the seller will offer and the lowest price the buyer will pay is called bid-ask-spread. The smaller this difference, the higher the demand will be.

- **Bull market**: A market in which investors expect the price of stocks to rise is a bull market. This generally occurs in more favorable economic conditions. The start of a bull market is an ideal time to buy, as you will profit from the increase. A simple way to remember this is if you think of a bull when it attacks; its horns gauge in an upwards motion—upwards is the direction of a bull market.

- **Bear market**: The opposite of a bull market is a bear market. It is a market condition where the stock prices are expected to fall. This generally occurs in less favorable economic conditions. Some investors may lose money in a bear market when the price of their stocks plummet, decreasing below the price they originally paid. Still, there are some strategies to make money in this market, such as going short. I will explain this later. Think of when a bear attacks, its claws swipe at you in a downwards motion, which is the direction of a bear market.

A piece of advice: *Wish for the Bull and plan for a Bear. You will have to face them both at some point. Be ready!*

- **Limit Order**: It is a command or instruction given to the broker to buy or sell a stock at a particular price that you set. A type of order that is set into action, only at a price based on buying or selling. If a trader wishes to buy a stock, for example, at $11.99, but at that moment, the actual market price of the stock is $12.20, they can set up an instruction to set the limit buy order as $11.99, and when the price of that particular stock reaches that threshold, it will be automatically purchased. It is convenient to use when you're confident the stock price will go to a certain level, whether up or down, and you have a strategy in place to avoid loss. Then, you can enter a trade at the price that works for you in your strategy. You can use multiple variations of this instruction based on your needs.

- **Market Order**: It is a type of order or instruction set into action as fast as possible for a speedy trade at the current price. Meaning, when you place a market order, your stocks will be sold, or new stocks will be bought immediately at the market price. Whatever price the stock holds at the time is the price at which it will be executed. You must be cautious with this one because it could get really tricky. If you are making a bulk transaction, then it is okay to use it sometimes, but for penny stocks—NEVER use it as you don't have any control over the price it executes at. Even the slightest fluctuation of a penny stock can have a significant impact. Therefore, I advise against penny stocks as a beginner.

- **Broker**: You must have heard me use this term frequently already. A broker is a professional who buys and sells on behalf of a client or company. For example, suppose you are busy and need assistance in managing your portfolio or require investment advice; in that case, you can hire a broker who can advise you and transact on your behalf. They may charge a fee to do so. This can be a person you get to speak to offering a more personal service transacting on your behalf. Or it can be an online company, trading platform, or website where you log on and trade for yourself. It is basically a person or company acting as a liaison between you and the exchange where the stocks are traded.

- **Day Order**: You will have stocks that you would like to buy or sell at a particular price. Since the value of stocks changes every day, you can set a day order. Brokers are given orders to buy or sell at a specific price that expires if it is not executed at the end of the day. Every day, new day orders are sent. If the order hasn't been carried out by the end of the day, it is automatically canceled as it didn't reach that price.

- **Volatility**: It refers to how fast the price of the stock fluctuates (rises and falls). It is an imbalance due to heavy one-sided trading. For instance, if the market is crashing down, everyone panics and starts selling their stocks. This one direction of selling and little to no buying causes volatility. The same phenomenon is true when everyone is buying, and no one is selling. You can easily see how volatile the stock pattern is by checking its graph over a period of time.

- **Going Long**: It is betting on the price of a stock increasing. Suppose you predict that a company's stock will increase in price; in that case, you are essentially betting you'll buy it at the current lower price and wait for it to rise to sell it for a higher price. You must be analytical and use this only when you're confident that profits are inevitable, according to your research, i.e., when you believe the price will increase.

- **Going Short**: An excellent move for a quick short-term profit. You are basically betting that the stock you sell will drop in price. This strategy is often used in a bearish market scenario. When your research concludes that the price of a particular stock could go down, as a trader, you can use this opportunity through a broker or an exchange and borrow a bunch of stocks. You can immediately sell them at that point (the higher price), and later when the price does fall lower as you predicted, you can then rebuy them at that time (at the lesser price) and return them to the broker who lent them to you. So, even though the price has gone down, you have still sold high and bought low because you could borrow stocks. You keep the differential profit from the trade. Pretty cool, isn't it? Remember, your research must be accurate for you to pull off this stunt.

- **Liquidity**: A term used when a stock is quickly being bought or sold—the more immediate the process, the more liquidity. Many traders make bulk trades quickly to enter and exit with profit. It refers to the ease with which an asset may be converted into cash without affecting its market price.

- **Averaging Down**: It's a situation when a trader, company, or broker buys additional stocks as its price lowers in hopes of decreasing the overall cost at which it was bought when looking at the average price of all trades.

For example, say you initially purchased stocks for $100, then the price falls to $90 and $80. When buying the same number of shares at each of these levels, the average price paid for the shares has reduced from the initial $100 down to $90. It is a way to increase your holdings, at the same time reducing the average cost paid.

- **Averaging Up:** It's simply the reverse of averaging down. It is when a broker or trader purchases additional shares of a company they already own at a higher price. It may sound odd at first: *why would you buy additional shares at a higher price?* Well, it's a strategy that enables one to average out the price of total owned stocks. It is often used when you believe the share price will increase rather than decrease. For some, it's an attractive strategy to increase their holdings in an upward market. For example, you buy stock ABC at $10 per share, and as the stock price rises, you buy further equal amounts at $15, $17, and $20 per share. This would then bring your average purchase price per share to $15.50. It is a way to increase your shareholding and to average out the purchase price.

- **Good till Canceled Order:** It is a form of a market order or instruction to buy or sell stocks. It remains valid unless the trade is made, or you can cancel the order at any time.

- **Market Capitalization (or Market Cap)**: It refers to the actual market price of a company, basically what the market thinks the company's value is. It is obtained by multiplying the price of one stock with the total number of available shares.

- **Trading Volume**: The total number of shares being traded at a particular time.

- **Float**: The number of shares that can be traded after subtracting the number of shares owned by the management or inside investors (usually company officers or employees). Generally, seek companies with very small public float because it provides more volatility.

- **Outstanding Shares**: It simply means the total number of shares in a company, including those available for the general public, along with the ones that are off-limits, such as those owned by company officers and insiders.

- **IPO**: It is an acronym for Initial Public Offering. It's a process where a company finally offers its shares in the marketplace for the first time. This is when a private company becomes a publicly-traded company, selling its shares to raise capital. It is often used to improve the business. It is basically when a company gets listed on the stock market for the first time.

- **Authorized Shares**: This is the specific number of shares or stocks that a company can trade. It is the minimum number of shares that a company is legally allowed to issue.

- **Secondary Offering**: An offering meant to sell more stocks to raise more money from the public. In short, the company can raise as much money from investors in exchange for shares, even after its stocks are available for trade after doing its IPO.

- **Blue-Chip Stocks**: These are the big players in the industry, companies that offer profitable growth and consistent dividends. Some known companies are Berkshire Hathaway, Larson, Toubro, Proctor and Gamble, Nestle, Amazon, Apple, Walmart, etc.

- **Dividend**: A portion of the company's earnings paid to shareholders—the people who own that company's stock.

It can be offered in any form, such as reward, cash, shares, etc., and is usually paid quarterly or annually. If you buy a stock that offers dividends, then this means you will be paid some reward, cash, shares, etc., for owning that stock. Dividend stocks can be great for earning regular passive income.

- **Market Index**: This is basically the measure representing the value of a batch of stocks. It is the collective subset of a stock market where stocks of multiple companies are held within different sectors. Thus, a group of different stocks is batched together in one fund. It will tell you the prices of all the stocks listed in it with precision. It is transparent and easy to calculate the value. You can invest in the market index by buying an index fund. They are categorized as mutual funds and Exchange Traded Funds. There are different types of funds out there, such as the S&P 500 index, DJIA, and Nasdaq composite index.

- **Exchange**: A place where different investments are traded. The most renowned in the United States are the Nasdaq and the New York Stock Exchange (NYSE).

- **Portfolio**: A collection of all your investments.

- **Margin**: Something that lets a person borrow money, magnifying their position to buy and sell more shares. It is tricky and risky, so I wouldn't recommend it to a beginner as there are chances of you making money and losing it all simultaneously.

- **Sector**: A group of stocks in the same industry. Or you can see them as many companies who serve the same industry such as medical, food, clothes, entertainment, technology, etc.

- **Stock Symbol or Ticker Symbol**: A string of unique characters consisting of letters or numbers as a name that represents a company on the exchange platform. It is the unique code used to identify a stock, which is usually a sort of abbreviation of the company name, much like your initials to identify yourself. For instance, Amazon trades under the symbol AMZN, Apple as AAPL, Tesla as TSLA, Berkshire Hathaway as BRK.A, etc. You get the gist.

- **Moving Average**: A routine indicator displayed on the stock chart. It's an average of a stock's price over a certain period of time. For example, a 30-day moving average of a stock is retained by referring to its 30-day value and finding the average. You can use it as a means of research to create a strategy for upcoming trends.

- **Price Quotes:** The price of a stock at a particular time. Traders and investors are always looking for an exact price quote to formulate a better strategy for profit.

- **Price Rally:** This is your dream term as an investor or trader. It means that the price of a stock is rising significantly at a quicker pace.

- **Dividend Yield:** It is a percentage financial ratio of dividend and stock price. It displays the dividend amount a company pays each year regarding its share price. For example, suppose a company's annual dividend payout to its shareholders is $2, and the stock trades at $20. In that case, the dividend yield is 10% ($2 ÷ $20). Don't confuse Dividend Yield with Dividend, though. The Dividend is the cash that lands in your pocket every quarter or every year, which the company pays out to its shareholder. The Dividend Yield is the annual percentage return in dividends on your investment. The higher the Dividend percentage yield, the more money you will be paid out in Dividends in relation to the cost of the share price. So, it can be an excellent way to compare stocks side-by-side to see which will provide the best return, i.e., the highest amount of money at the lowest cost.

- **Arbitrage:** It means buying and selling the same stock on different platforms to make a quick profit. Stock prices can differ on various platforms, much like the same pair of trainers can sell for different prices at different stores. Taking advantage of the location, platform, or other factors, traders could buy stock from one place at a specific price and sell it at another place at a higher price to make a quick profit. For example, if a stock is priced at $13.99 on platform A and $14.45 on platform B, you can buy the stock from A and sell it on B. You will keep $0.46 as a profit—provided the number of stocks bought and sold remains the same. At a hundred stocks, that is a quick profit of $46.

- **Beta:** It is the measure of stocks' relation to the overall market. The higher the beta, the more risk, but it also enables the probability of a higher profit. Beta is a measure of volatility or systematic risk of a portfolio compared to the market as a whole.

- **Pink Sheet Stocks or Penny Stocks**: Usually, these are the penny stocks of a smaller company, with the price of each stock being $5 or less. They are defined by the Securities and Exchange Commission (SEC) as stocks with a market cap of less than $250 million. Think of them as cheap stocks. They remain unavailable on major platforms like NYSE or Nasdaq. Sometimes, also referred to as over-the-counter stocks. As a beginner, it is best to stay away from trading these until you are more experienced. The slightest price fluctuations can have devastating effects, and this market is full of scams.

- **Alpha**: It's your relative return on investment in proportion to the overall market. It lets you know if a stock has consistently performed well against its beta predictions. It is also a measure of risk. You will know the performance ratio of stock by understanding its Alpha value.

You can only learn a language by speaking it regularly. It is easier to get the hang of it if you insert these terms in your vocabulary while referring to the stock market. Although you do not need to know all these terms, many of them will come in handy. Investing in stocks is pretty easy, but you will often come across these terms when you reach a certain point, and that point may be from the very beginning. You should be prepared for uncertainty, is what they say in the stock market.

When you read the Wall Street Journal, watch the news, listen to top stock investors, attend seminars, or seek mentors, you will need to know these terms to avoid being left out. Of course, there are more terms besides the ones mentioned in this chapter. Still, these will set a foundation on which you can start building a pillar of knowledge and experience.

Start learning these basic stock market terms and move on to the next chapter, where I will explain how to get into the stock market game. But, before that, let's review what we just learned in this chapter.

SUMMARY

1. To fall in love with the stock market, you must learn to speak the same language.

2. Learning the standard terms of the stock market will help you rectify the language and gain the upper hand when an opportunity presents itself. In addition, you will have a better understanding of the environment being discussed.

3. Do not doubt the importance of learning the language of the stock market. You will truly be surrounded by pros and high-performance players in the game. To keep up, understanding these terms is a prerequisite.

4. You now have some common terminologies people in the stock market use. Learn them thoroughly, research them further, speak a more fluent language, and have a better understanding. Then, with your new, not-so-foreign language, impress your friends and family!

CHAPTER 3

STEP 2

GETTING INTO THE GAME

> *"The stock market is the story of cycles and the*
> *human behaviour that is responsible for*
> *overreactions in both directions."*
>
> **– Seth Klarman**

L earning the language of the stock market may have built a little bit of confidence within you. With that current boost, you should easily be able to get into the game and get set up for success. This chapter will help you get started as quickly as possible and direct you on what you will need to get set up to start trading. You have successfully completed the first step, and now, it is time to take the second step on the road to reaping the full benefit of your hard-earned money. In the beginning, you should probably do it on your own instead of using a broker; this way, you will learn more.

You will save on the fees that go into the pocket of the broker or account manager—it is better to find an online broker application or software and follow each step yourself to be aware of the entire process. We will start small and slow—no need to rush into anything! We want to operate on a very low-risk basis in the beginning.

OPENING YOUR FIRST BANK ACCOUNT

To initialize your investments, you need to open a simple bank account. If you're not 18 years old yet, you will need your parent's supervision and guidance when it comes to opening a bank account, whether it's a checking or savings account. There is a difference between the two; so, go with the one more tailored to your needs. Checking accounts might be the most straightforward option because you have access to the money very easily. You get easy ATM transactions, online access, debit card usage, and it is excellent for everyday use. Although, there might be certain charges with this account, like when you don't maintain the minimum balance in your bank account or use another bank's ATM to withdraw money from your bank. This is true for your savings account as well. However, your savings account is more of a long-term account where the interest rates are higher. You put your money in with the vision of later using it to buy a car or go on a relaxing vacation, or better yet, invest in the stock market!

There might be distractions along your way as a teen where you may be enticed to make an impulse or careless purchase of expensive branded clothing, accessories, or other attractive things. You can choose a savings account to prevent that from happening, as it provides limited access to its users. That's why most teens opt for a savings account in the same bank their parents are subscribed to. Opening a savings account might be a good idea because it limits how much you can withdraw, keeping your money safe from unwanted reckless expenditures. If you're not an impulse buyer, then you can also go ahead with the checking account. But I encourage you to move ahead with a savings account first; it holds many benefits. Whichever you select, ensure it allows making payments, such as wire transfers, to top up your investment account. This is the most crucial feature you need from the account. Once you have a bank account, the next step is your investment account, allowing you to get to the exciting part—trading!

THREE TYPES OF INVESTMENT ACCOUNTS

The title might have surprised you, as most people are unaware of the different options out there. This isn't a subject taught in high school. Yes, there are different types of investment accounts for you to choose from. Let us review them one by one, so you can choose the best one for yourself.

- **Standard Brokerage Account**: This type of account gives you easy access to various kinds of investments. These include stocks, exchange-traded funds (ETFs), bonds, mutual funds, and more. This account is also sometimes referred to as a non-retirement account or a taxable brokerage account. At every point while using this account, if you earn any interest or dividends from your investment, or if you gain a profit by selling your holdings, you are subjected to pay the tax. According to an article on nerdwallet.com, it was stated: *"With a non-retirement account you have a choice in how it is owned: first, Individual taxable brokerage account: Opened by an individual who retains ownership of the account and will be solely responsible for the taxes generated in the account. Second, Joint taxable brokerage account: An account shared by two or more people — typically spouses, but it can be opened with anyone, even a non-relative."*

  If you decide to go ahead with the standard brokerage account, you will choose from one of these two subtypes. You can choose a cash account or a margin account. Most investors choose a cash account as it enables you to use the cash you deposit in your account to buy your investments. If you're looking to borrow money from a broker to buy your investments, you should most likely go ahead with a margin account. I wouldn't recommend you look into margin trading yet; it is reserved for advanced traders who have witnessed the market's ups and downs and are willing to take and fully understand the risk. As a beginner, start with a cash account and work your way up to a margin account.

There are a few criteria for you to be eligible to open a standard brokerage account. First, you must be 18 years old or above. Second, you should have a tax ID number or a social security number. Finally, the amount of money you can deposit into the taxable brokerage account has no upper limit, although you will have to pay tax after gaining a profit when selling your assets or if they have increased in value.

Webull, Interactive brokers, Ameritrade, etc., are some options available for online brokerage firms. Check out www.jp-clarke.com/resources, where I have put together some very useful resources, including links to various websites & brokerages, budgeting & goal-setting tools, free downloads, and other handy information to help get you started on your investment journey.

- **Investment Account for Kids**: This account is made for teenagers who want to invest, though you must be at least 18 years old to open one. For early starters who wish to defy the age barriers, there are ways to get around this and have an account. A custodial brokerage account could be a viable solution for those of you who aren't 18 yet. The two types of custodial accounts available are the Uniform Transfers to Minors Act (UTMA) and the Uniform Gift to Minors Act (UGMA). Here, the control remains with the custodian adult, parent, or guardian, who acts as a caretaker of the account.

Once the young teen reaches the required age, the account and the assets can be transferred to them. In both UTMA and UGMA, you can hold all the usual investments such as stocks, mutual funds, bonds, etc. The only upside of having a UTMA account is that it enables you to buy and hold real estate as well. Ensure you utilize all the money in the account as it cannot be transferred to any other beneficiary.

If you earn and have your own income, there is an option for a custodial Roth or traditional IRA. It works similarly; your parent or guardian will hold the account until you reach the appropriate age and can then transfer the assets to you.

- **Retirement Account**: A retirement account such as an IRA is the same as the usual brokerage account; you get to buy and sell all the common investments. It is basically a retirement plan which is something you need to think about in your earlier years. Now is a perfect time! The only difference is in the manner in which this account is taxed. Types of retirement accounts are traditional IRA and Roth IRA. Investing becomes more organized and strategic if you do it through a Roth IRA. However, only people with earned income are allowed to open an IRA. Additionally, there is a maximum to how much you may invest into an IRA. At the time of publishing, for people below 50 years old, it's almost $6000, and for people older than 50, it's $7000.

These are the three types of investment accounts available. You can go ahead and choose the one that fulfills your requirements. I can guess that things are getting a little overwhelming with all the options and sub-options. But I entrust you to choose an account and just get started. Feel free to discuss these options with your parents or guardians to determine which works best for your situation. Reach out to our Facebook community (www.facebook.com/groups/investingbeginner) or me if you have any questions. Do not let the complexity hold you back and delay your financial freedom. This is where you seek help from your parents or guardian because most accounts will require their consent and approval.

CHOOSING THE RIGHT ONLINE BROKER

Once you have decided which account works best for you, it is time to take the next step. A long time ago, it was much harder actually to invest in stocks. It was usually done over the phone or in-person with a broker. We do, however, live in the twenty-first century, and there are tons of online applications where you can open an account using a web-based brokerage to start investing. Now, you can invest from the comfort of your home, online on your computer, or an app on your smartphone! Now you've decided on the type of account you wish to open, you can start your journey, investing in stocks to achieve financial independence.

Since minors (below the age of 18 or 21 depending on your state) are not allowed to own an account, you should carefully find brokers that permit a custodial account. A custodial account would mean you own the assets within that account, but your parent or guardian would control the investments within it until you have reached the required age. Here is a checklist to consider for an account.

- Find online brokers that charge $0 as trading fees.

- A low balance or $0 minimum balance account is favorable.

- It should allow the option of fractional shares.

Here is a list of the different online brokers and applications you could investigate (all links available at www.jp-clarke.com/resources). Of course, each has advantages and disadvantages, but they all do the same thing—they assist you in getting started in the stock market.

- **Charles Schwab**: According to a Wikipedia article, Charles Schwab Corporation is an American multinational financial services company owned by Bank of America. It offers banking, commercial banking, an electronic trading platform, and wealth management advisory services to retail and institutional clients. It has a total of 360 branches across the United States and the United Kingdom. Charles Schwab is one of the best choices for beginners as there are no account opening or maintenance fees. There is no minimum balance to maintain either. You can open an account for free and start trading. It is also the world's third-largest asset manager, behind Blackrock and Vanguard. The company was founded in 1971 and has been around ever since. It's been over 50 years.

  Setting up your account on Charles Schwab is an easy 10-minute process. Simply click on "Open Account" through the website and follow their step-by-step process in getting the account opened and topped up with some funds to start investing with.

- **Stockpile:** It's an online brokerage platform that allows both individual brokerage accounts and custodial accounts. There is no annual fee on this platform, and the trading fee is less than a dollar, one of the most affordable in the industry. Simply create and fund your account and choose the stocks that resonate with you or those you find worthy (we will get into this later). You can link your bank account or use a debit card as well for fund transfers. Stockpile offers over 4000 plus stocks and ETFs, including every S&P 500.

- **Ally Invest**: It's an easy solution for all beginners. It offers easy-to-use tools and an interactive platform with zero minimum account and transactional fees. There are no commission fees on all eligible US stock options and ETFs. There are also some tremendously robust tools available that could help you in your research. However, there is a small transactional fee for mutual funds. It is a one-stop solution to all the common types of investments such as stocks, bonds, mutual funds, ETFs, options, forex, and even penny stocks. You should also know that Ally Invest is an entirely online platform with no physical branches.

- **E-Trade:** It is another financial corporation that is a subsidiary of Morgan Stanley. According to Wikipedia, it's an electronic trading platform for all your financial assets such as common stocks, preferred stocks, exchange-traded funds, futures contracts, options, mutual funds, and fixed-income investments. E-Trade is a popular choice and holds many benefits for investors. While starting out, it is good to have things in perspective and sort a few backups as well. Here, you can trade by yourself or even seek help or guidance from a professional. Experienced traders and an inventory of knowledge are always at your disposal with E-Trade to keep you on the frontlines. There are several tools available to help you keep track of your portfolio, analyze the market data from a very sharp angle, and create an action plan for your retirement. Their customers are happy with their service, and there are tons of online resources like FAQs, forums, etc.

- **TD Ameritrade:** It's also a brokerage company that offers financial asset management services for all the investment options out there. It requires no minimum balance, no commission fees, and some free data to perform your research. There are almost 300 branches, just in case you need some face-to-face assistance. The platform is fairly straightforward to use, and the tools they provide are beneficial as well, along with comprehensive data. Schwab and Ameritrade are now part of one company. They work together to provide a seamless experience for their investors and users by combining their strengths and incorporating them into a single platform.

- **Loved Investing:** It's a brokerage firm that provides UTMA accounts (Uniform Transfers to Minor Act). It provides you with all the standard features, including some additional features that you will find compelling. For example, there is an option of setting goals which can be very handy. The already inserted goal options are things such as college, first car, etc. You can insert any goal you like, and then a savings plan to meet that goal will be set. It automatically deducts money from your account and invests it so that, in the end, you meet your goals. Not very handy for a custodial account because of the automation, but when used wisely, you can definitely see some potential, and it is a great way to start as a beginner.

  Another great feature that I find interesting is the 'share' feature. In this, you can send money or shares to your friends and family. The send and receive features allow you to transfer or receive shares from your parents, friends, etc. You can even arrange the transfer for a special birthday or as a gift to your loved ones, hence the name. The information provided is not a complete expanded edition, but the interface is clean and easy to navigate.

- **Fidelity:** It offers commission-free trading and broker accounts. Even if you're planning on becoming a day trader or a long-term investor, this platform is a good choice for both. No transactional or minimum account balance fees, even for mutual funds. Furthermore, it offers fractional shares trading of over 7000+ US ETF stocks. For your convenience and guidance, Fidelity provides you with a Robo-advisor. It is filled with educational content and research materials to aid in your analysis and strategy formulation. Its 'news and research' tab displays real-time investment prices and stock market trends. Active traders benefit from a great online platform and mobile app.

There are multiple investing and retirement tools as well. One thing that should be considered here is that, although there is no charge or fee for a smaller account, once the balance crosses $10,000, it carries a 0.35% annual fee at the time of publishing.

That's it; you're now officially a part of the game of stocks and are up against the world. Pump up your spirits and keep your mind open. Follow the process and see what bright future you hold. Things have gotten a little technical in this chapter, and we learned a lot of stuff here, but the results are worth the read. Let us review the chapter to get that memory jogging, shall we?

SUMMARY

1. Christon "The Truth" Jones spent his free time trading stocks and earned $78,000 in one trade in just a few short months. He demonstrated that nothing is impossible in this world, and there is no age barrier to becoming successful. If he can, you can, and you will!

2. Open your first bank account.

3. Choose your investment account type. The three different types of investment accounts are Standard Brokerage Account, Investment Account for Kids, and a Retirement Account.

4. Research and choose your online broker wisely; the list includes Charles Schwab, Stockpile, E-Trade, Ally Invest, TD Ameritrade, Loved Investing, and Fidelity. Of course, there are more, but these are my favorite options for beginners. All links are available at www.jp-clarke.com/resources.

CHAPTER 4

STEP 3

WRAPPING YOUR HEAD AROUND THE BASICS

"Compounding is the eighth wonder of the world. He who understands it, earns it. He who doesn't, pays it."

– Albert Einstein

After learning the language, and before you start buying shares, it is wise to learn about the stock market as a whole. You now own an account, and I can understand your anxious excitement. You want to get in there and make some money, don't you? Remember, haste is a weapon of evil. It is vital that you first wrap your head around the stock market basics and how it works. If you understand it well, you will be prepared for what's coming. This chapter will teach you everything you need to know about the stock market. If you're wondering why the world of stocks exists in the first place, then let me clear that up first.

You must have heard the famous rags to riches stories of the biggest companies starting from a garage, a small apartment, or a dorm room. Like Apple, Amazon, Microsoft, Facebook, Google, Alibaba, and many more, the greatest giants in the market didn't exist 50 years ago. Today, they are the biggest companies on the face of the earth. How did that happen? Most of these companies were launched as small private entities by entrepreneurs and visionaries who wanted to change the world. To transform their crazy ideas into operational companies, buying raw materials, leasing office space and hiring employees were obviously inescapable.

Furthermore, to expand internationally on such a magnitude within a few years requires a massive flow of capital, i.e., money. Where do you think that much money came from? Initially, the entrepreneurs invested their own livelihood and personal savings to breathe life into their dreams. Then, they may have sought help from the people they know, relatives, and family. Finally, when the need for capital grew, angel investors and venture capital firms were also included in the process to fund the idea.

Investors and people who believed that these start-ups would one day rule the world joined forces to lend a hand. When the demand increased and the supply was limited, these companies went under an IPO (Initial Public Offering) to expand further. They enabled ordinary people to invest their money in exchange for a portion of ownership in the company. With a promise that, whenever the company grows its assets and net value, all the investors will be benefitted as a result. The need to securely carry out such transactions seeded the birth of the stock market. That is why companies sell their shares; they get the money to expand, and investors gain an additional source of income. Your investment is fuelling a company and the economy to grow exponentially. That makes you a significant contributor as a respectable citizen. You are not just gaining a profit in cash; you are making the world a better place in which to live. That's a much greater reward of being an investor.

Wall Street trader, Martin Schwartz, said, *"I always laugh at people who keep saying, 'I've never met a rich technician' I love that! It's such an arrogant, nonsensical response. I used the fundamentals for nine years and got rich as a technician."* When you get your fundamentals right, it is easy to recognize complex structures. That's what we are going to master today!

WHAT IS THE STOCK MARKET?

The stock market is where investors and companies unite to buy and sell shares in the public domain. If you know anything about stocks, you've probably heard of the New York Stock Exchange (NYSE) or Nasdaq; that's where all the action occurs. Companies usually own stocks in the exchange, and they are priced at a particular value. What does buying a stock mean? When you buy a company's stock, you are investing in that particular company. It's like becoming an owner. Based on your research, you are waiting for that company to thrive and make more money. This will, in turn, make you more money because you are an investor. The Stock Market is, basically, like an auction. You are there to buy or sell a stock. The general rule of thumb is, *buy a stock when it is low, wait until it increases in value, sell the stock, and make a profit—* pretty simple. Buy low, sell high is the aim of the game!

We have been blessed with technology in the 21st century, allowing us to invest from the convenience of our own homes. You don't even need to get dressed and go out; everything you need is present at your fingertips. The stock market has also become an electronic medium where you can invest in anything from anywhere. Multiple software and platforms allow you to do so, as discussed in the previous chapter.

Anyone can start investing, and everyone has a fair chance to succeed. When you start buying and selling stocks, you're in the same league as professional investors who are trying to build long-term wealth with the same tools you have. A stock market platform is mandatory because it is challenging to keep track of every company's stock. With this, you can gain instant insight into all the latest trends, news, companies, profits, and losses. The stock market displays an exact value of the share and its performance; the same is referred to by the entire market. So, when people make a fuss over the stock market and say that it has gone up or down, they mean that the shares' value has decreased or increased, respectively. These movements in the value of shares dictate whether investors will suffer losses or gain profits.

The stock market is filled with success stories, one of which is Brandon Fleisher, who started investing when he was in high school. A 17-year-old boy fell in love with investing and has gained the ability to comprehensively find stocks to gain profit. He is known for tripling his investments within two years to $147,000! With his extensive knowledge, he is helping other amateur traders to become professional investors. While being a high school senior, he managed to earn almost $1.5 million. Scottish football manager, Steve Clarke, said, *"Do more of what works and less of what doesn't."* It's excellent advice that applies to investing as well.

UNDERSTANDING THE STOCK MARKET

Now you know what the stock market is, let's move on and dive deep to understand how it works. In simple terms, buyers and sellers negotiate the price of a stock; hence, trade is made. Various companies undergo the process of Initial Public Offering (IPO), where they list their stocks for exchange on Nasdaq and NYSE. When investors find these companies and see growth potential, they purchase their stocks. It helps the company to raise money and grow its business. The exchange keeps track of every share, its available supply, and the required demand. The investors can then trade the stocks to make a quick profit or hold them for a period hoping for the company to increase its value. There are four kinds of investments you can make while trading in stocks:

- **Individual shares**: These are the good old stocks or pieces of ownership in the company that you invest in. Each stock is an individual share. You can buy them, then sell them for a profit or wait for the company to increase the value of its assets and sell for an even higher profit. For instance, purchasing a stock for 150 dollars and then holding on to it, and years later, it could be ten times more valuable when the company has increased in value.

- **Fractional Shares**: If you don't have that much money to buy an entire share, you can instead choose a different approach. Fractional shares are small chunks of the same share. Instead of $150, you can get a fractional share for as little as $5. That's a great way to start. This could get you into your favorite company, say, Tesla, Disney, Apple, etc.

- **Exchange-Traded Funds or ETFs**: It is like a complete package of contentment. It tracks an index, commodity, industry, or other assets. It usually contains a bundle of different types of investments in one place, such as stocks, commodities, bonds, or a mixture of these. As a result, you can invest with little money, and it diversifies your amount between the assets within the fund. The SPDR S&P 500 ETF (SPY) is a popular example that tracks the index known as the S&P 500. ETFs are usually much more cost-effective, with fewer broker commissions.

- **Index funds**: If you feel that stocks are riskier and there is a massive chance that the market could be volatile (go up and down), and you don't want to take the risk, you can invest your money in an index fund. It is a type of mutual fund or ETF put together to track components of a financial market index. Generally, over some time, they usually only go up. Because of such low-risk tolerance, most beginners only invest in index funds as they are seen as a safe investment. I would recommend you incorporate an index fund into your investment portfolio, such as the S&P 500.

To help explain the stock market, a simple trade between two traders is made when one person wishes to sell their owned shares, and the other seeks to buy them. The seller will provide the buyer with an asking price. The buyer counter proposes with a bid (it is the maximum price the buyer is willing to pay for the stocks, usually lower than the asking price). It is similar to how you bargain for goods at a market stall. In order for the trade to take place, either the buyer has to increase their bid to the asking price or the seller has to decrease their asking price to match the bid. In any case, the difference between the asking price and the bid is called bid-ask-spread. Unlike bargaining at a market stall, usually for $1 or more, the bid-ask spread is generally only a couple of cents. You won't have to complete any complicated calculations because the majority of the work will be done by electronic computer algorithms. All these values will be automatically present on your broker's website or application.

You may have heard from your peers or relatives that the stock market involves risk. That's a fact, but along with risk, there is also an opportunity to become very wealthy. Every time you leave your house, your face loads of risks in your daily life. Does that mean you will never leave your home? No, of course not. If you employ the proper strategies at the appropriate moment, you will prosper with incredible profits and low long-term risks. There is a strategy that people have used lately, called day trading, to make a quick buck. That is a risky strategy and is not recommended for beginners. It has been proven on more than one occasion that long-term vision beats short-term profits. There are more chances that you will end up becoming successful by holding stocks over some time. Day trading may not be for you; the stress and burden of suffering a daily loss can be too much for beginners. Don't get me wrong, some people make quite a lot of money using this method, but that doesn't mean that what works for them will work for you. Stay invested and face the ups and downs of the market; in the end, you will be glad you did.

When you invest, the market index will tell you how your investments are doing. Did you make a profit? Did you lose money? The market index will be your best friend to achieve financial independence. The stock market correction occurs slowly, typically when the market drops by 10% or more. If you hear of a stock market crash, that's a disaster! It means that the value of the stocks has quickly dropped significantly. There is no need to panic, though; it has been researched that a bull market lasts longer than a bear market. So, if things are bad, it could be a good idea to buy as many stocks as you can because things will change soon. Have patience, and you shall reap the benefits in cash. You can think of a stock market crash as a flash sale, an opportunity to buy low. But always refer to your research to ensure those you are purchasing have future growth potential.

Justin Brosseau is a millennial who cracked the headlines in 2015 when he managed to make 250% returns on his stock investments. That's huge! At the time, he was just 16 years old when he invested all his money in the stock market, which was only $650. He purchased stocks of the following three companies: United Airlines (UAL), Citi (C), and GE (GE). The returns he witnessed were outstanding for a boy of his age. He then continued to invest heavily into stocks, and seven years down the line, he increased his returns by 19-fold. According to TradeVeda, *"Justin's interest in stock trading began in his sophomore year at Neuqua Valley High School. His teacher had given them the assignment to create mock stocks. For the project, Justin picked United Airlines, which he studied its finances till he felt comfortable with it.*

He then convinced his dad to co-sign a Scottrade account and bought United shares at $4 a share in 2009. He sold the stake in 2014 at $41. Justin prefers long-term trading. First, he conducts extensive homework on the company by considering yardsticks like profits, sales, and earnings per share. He also considers the company's capital spending to give a measure of its future. According to Justin, there is always a 'win some and lose some situation,' keeping in mind that he invested in other companies apart from Netflix (NFLX), Apple (AAPL), and Disney (DIS), but did not fare too well."

American businessman, Bill Lipschutz, said, *"If most traders would learn to sit on their hands 50 percent of the time, they would make a lot more money."* It would have been boring yet profitable in the stock market if humans were born without emotions. Instead, things get exciting and lively because we all have an impulse to make reckless decisions. When it comes to investing money, people are fearful and agitated. Nobody wants to suffer a heavy loss, and everybody is hoping for a quick gigantic profit. You are probably thinking the same too. Decision-making is more of an emotional instinct rather than a rational one. When people are worried and intimidated by an irregular stock movement or a complete crash, they panic and start selling every last share they own to keep the loss to a minimum. In the opposite circumstance, the same is true. When the stock value seems to be increasing, they buy as many as they can to gain profits.

The most dominant sentiments, known as greed and fear, play an influential role in the world of stocks. Behaviors enforce action and are thus described by a result. No wonder the mere thought of investing in the stock market scares you. When beginners enter the market with limited knowledge, they have likely already heard all the horrifying stories about people who lost a fortune in stocks. Everyone around them, including their relatives and peers, warned about the harmful damage it could inflict upon them. That generates implausible fear of failure. Everyone who enters the realm of the stock market has these two emotions within them: the greed of making tremendous money in the shortest time or the fear of losing the money in hand, playing it too safe to even make a profit. In the midst, those with the passion for creating a fortune backed by the desire to learn and the discipline to wait - win!

INVESTMENT DIVERSIFICATION

Every investor is subjected to both the bear and the bull market. Based on the risk tolerance, there is a need to avoid additional damage to the existing portfolios. Investors use multiple strategies to elude significant loss, one of which is diversification. This is a topic of discussion; everyone has their own perspective about diversifying their investments. Some apply that diversifying is essential as a means of protection and growth stability.

Conversely, some believe that prime diversification could reduce profits. Nobody is right or wrong here. It all depends upon your knowledge, experience, and personal goals. You must understand what you really want for your career as an investor. Does diversifying work for you? If yes, then how much of it?

Diversifying means that an investor or trader invests in a bunch of stocks from various companies or industries. Let's say instead of diversifying, you choose to find one company that you think will make you rich and invest all your money into it. Of course, the money invested in this is greater, and thus, the returns gained may be spectacular, but you also risk losing it all if that company fails. Now, let's assume you choose to diversify and invest in multiple companies within the same industry, say in the oil & gas industry. You are diversifying, hoping to even out the average loss if one or two companies suffered a significant drop in value. You may diversify in this industry by buying shares of established companies that provide a gradual increase in annual returns; you buy a few from companies that offer steady dividends and some from newly established companies with rapid growth. In both the above scenarios, you are still only investing in one industry. If this industry takes a dive, for instance, oil & gas being replaced by renewable energy, you are not really fully diversified.

As attractive as it sounds, I wouldn't recommend either one of the two options mentioned above. There is a third route that could lead you to stability, protection, as well as remarkable growth and profit. This route offers better diversification. In this strategy, you will choose a few great companies that will pay you handsome returns and dividends across multiple industries which are not related. Invest heavily in them. It could be anywhere between 4 to 15 companies, but start small and build from there. These will be the result of your intense research. It basically means that you find a few companies from multiple industries and invest in them to diversify your portfolio. For instance, instead of diversifying your investments between five companies in one or two industries, you can find 10-15 companies from 5-10 industries (say technology, entertainment, medical, food, clothing, renewable energy, etc.) and invest in them.

This way, you protect yourself if a few companies suffer losses or even if a few industries suffer losses. Do not simply invest in the first companies you come across. Instead, find out which companies could fulfill your milestones and goals.

Over time, you can even invest in a new company as you see growth potential, but this selected batch will be your go-to option.

Diversifying your portfolio is crucial, but know how much of it is manageable. Regardless of market setbacks, you can stay protected and take less risk while making a profit. One more problem you can face is that building a portfolio of diversified individual stocks is not an easy task. It requires enormous research and a lot of time, especially in the beginning. To ensure you do not lose precious time, there is the option of mutual funds or ETFs. As mentioned before, Exchange Traded Funds or index funds are a batch of multiple investment stocks. You will recall we covered the Market Index in previous chapters, which tells you the price of a group of stocks. It is usually categorized by sectors; you can find the definition of it in chapter two. Your investments will automatically be diversified if you invest in one fund. You don't have to put up with the trouble of finding 15 good companies; you can instead research that one particular fund and start investing. Consider this, for example, when you invest in the S&P 500 index, you invest in all 500 companies included in it. Index funds are usually the safest options out there.

You can also level up and insert both index funds and individual stocks in one portfolio. By doing so, you are under the protection of secured index funds while taking risks with individual stocks that could turn into a rewarding strategy.

Tip: *When starting out, invest most of your money in index funds and a small portion in individual stocks. For instance, 80%-90% in the index fund and 20%-10% in the individual stocks.*

There you have it, the basic understanding of what the stock market is and how it operates. Now that you have this information, you can go on to pick your investments, which we will examine in the next chapter. Let's review everything we learned in this chapter before moving on.

SUMMARY

1. Haste is a weapon of evil. Therefore, it is vital you first wrap your head around the stock market basics before you rush in and start buying stocks that you know nothing about.

2. The stock market came into existence because companies needed capital to expand their business. After using the cash from personal savings and the people around them, business owners turned towards angel investors and firms. When the need for more capital increased, they went under an IPO and availed their shares to the general public in exchange for a portion of their company's ownership.

3. When you get your fundamentals right, it is easy to recognize complex structures—focus on the principle.

4. The stock market is where investors and companies unite to buy and sell shares in the public domain.

5. The Nasdaq, as well as the New York Stock Exchange (NYSE), is where all the action takes place.

6. The Stock Market is, basically, like an auction. You are there to buy or sell a stock. The general rule of thumb is; buy low, sell high.

7. A stock market platform is mandatory because it is challenging to keep track of every company's stock. With this, you can gain instant ingress to all the latest trends, news, companies, profits, and losses.

8. The four kinds of investments are Individual Shares, Fractional Shares, Exchange Trading Funds or ETFs, and Index Funds.

9. The market index will be your best friend to achieve financial independence. Investing in index funds could be a good starting point for a beginner.

10. The most dominant sentiments, known as greed and fear, play a powerful role in the world of stocks.

11. Investors use multiple strategies to elude significant loss, one of which is diversification. It means an investor or a trader invests in many stocks from various companies, hoping to even out the average loss if one or two of the stocks owned suffer a significant drop in value.

12. Insert both index funds and individual stocks in one portfolio for a higher profit, and lower risk.

CHAPTER 5

STEP 4

DECIDING YOUR INVESTMENTS

> *"It's not whether you're right or wrong that's important; it is how much money you make when you're right and how much money you lose when you're wrong."*
>
> **– George Soros**

U nderstanding what the stock market is and how it works brought you closer to your consequent goal of becoming financially independent. Your account is ready, and your knowledge is in great shape. All you need now is to know how to decide your investments. Meaning, you should have a solid strategy to research the best stocks that suit your needs and passions. This chapter is the 4th step in the 7-step process of making you a financially independent person. It will be focused entirely on providing you with a concrete research strategy in helping you decide the best investments.

As Benjamin Franklin once said, *"An investment in knowledge pays the best interest."* Before we drill down into the exact research methods, let's first understand some basic rules and principles to follow, which I call "The 10 Commandments for Beginners."

THE 10 COMMANDMENTS FOR BEGINNERS

When you set out to find some great investments, there are a few rules that you should be aware of. You should be wise to make them your own and follow through. Note them down and understand the importance they each carry. Let's get started.

1. **Know what the companies do**: It is not just enough to see a social media post and decide to invest in a particular company. If you want to be sure about your profits, take a step forward and get a copy of the annual report corresponding to the company you want to invest in. According to TeenVestor, *"an annual report is a document used by most public companies to disclose the corporate information to their stockholders. It is usually a state-of-the-company report, including an opening letter from the Chief Executive Officer, financial data, results of operations, market segment information, new product plans, subsidiary activities, and research and development activities on future programs."* An annual report will provide you with thorough information that will be beneficial for your decision-making process. You will know precisely what the company is doing currently and its future goals. It is pretty easy to get the annual report from a Google search or directly from the company. It is usually available on their website in the investor's section.

   If you cannot find the PDF there, you can also contact them directly through the website and ask for a physical copy of the annual report. Everything mentioned in the report from the company is official and accurate erudition. Suppose you wish to get a more detailed version of a company's annual report and financial performance. In that case, you can get the 10-K report. It is a more comprehensive view of the report which investors and analysts use. You may find it on the SEC's website or by doing a Google search. If you understand the basics, you should be okay with the annual report. Company financials are also available on finance sites such as Yahoo Finance and many others.

2. **Experiment with dummy accounts:** If you're unsure about trading real money at first, create a dummy or virtual account and learn to trade with virtual money. Setting up a separate virtual account will enable you to learn risk-free with real stocks in real-time, and the money is not actually coming out of your pocket, so you have nothing to lose. Many platforms offer a virtual trading account to practice in the stock market world for free, and you could make it more enjoyable by competing with your friends to see who makes the most money! Then, once you get the required confidence within you, trade with real money. Here are a few platforms that offer virtual accounts: TeenVestor, TD Bank's Virtual Stock Market, MarketWatch Virtual Stock Exchange, Stock Game, Wall Street Survivor, How the Market Works, etc.; all links are available at www.jp-clarke.com/resources.

John Ducan started learning with virtual accounts when he was only nine years old. After reaching thirteen, he started trading by opening a live trading account through an online broker. He learned about the stock market and which stocks he could make money on, using the virtual platform first, which led him to make a lot of money on the live platform with real money. In fact, most young investor millionaires first started learning using a virtual trade account.

3. **Ignore the scammers:** While on your journey to create wealth and abundance, you will encounter many scammers who promise ridiculous profits and steal your money. If the returns they promise are insanely high compared to what the research has proven the company offers annually, then run as fast as you can away from them. If it is too good to be true, think twice, it usually is. Unless you believe the result is 100% accurate, do not let other people handle your

money. The market is never stationary; not all returns are consistent throughout the year. If anyone is telling you otherwise, be mindful that it could be a scam. There are people and illegitimate companies or brokers who take advantage of beginners, asking them to invest immediately by painting a rosy picture of how much money they will make. They will apply a lot of pressure for you to commit, do not fall for the trap. Do your homework, learn about them, only then decide whether to invest or not.

4. **Invest in the business you understand**: This is the most obvious one. I have mentioned it previously, but it is worth highlighting as most people don't seem to get it. For some reason, people believe that in the stock market, the things they don't understand are better and more profitable. So, they invest in them, hoping for huge gains. Sometimes, they get lucky and earn a little profit here and there, but almost everybody loses money when they try to capitalize on things beyond their understanding. If you still want to get in, knowing that you could miss an opportunity if you don't, then take time to learn about that business first. Warren Buffett said, *"The best investment you can ever make is an investment in yourself. The more you learn, the more you'll earn."* You should invest in yourself because the more knowledge you have about a business, the more chances you have of being competent about it. For example, suppose you know nothing about a company or assume you know about it when you really don't; in that case, you will likely lose money on that investment. Another reason is that you need to make better, intelligent decisions about your investments, and thus, exhaustive knowledge is mandatory. Also, you will be more motivated to learn and invest in something you understand and find interesting instead of something you don't understand or do not like.

5. **Don't put all your eggs in one basket by investing everything in 1-2 companies:** When we talked about

diversifying your portfolio, we mentioned this briefly. If you place all of your money into one stock, you risk losing it all if it goes down, but if you split it out among three or four stocks, your chances of losing money are reduced. Of course, as a beginner, you need to start with one stock and then build from there. Have at least three or four solid companies that could provide handsome annual returns and dividends. Make sure to choose from different industries to not lose it all if one goes down. Be careful, though, as mentioned before, know how much diversification is manageable by you. Don't go crazy with investing in 30-40 companies, as initially, your funds are limited. When you get into the stock world, you will see profitable companies all over the place and feel an itchy sensation to invest in all of them—cool your jets.

6. **Invest only in those with a solid track record:** This will enable you to stay in the game for the long term, especially when you're just starting. Once you complete your research, which we will get into later, invest in only promising companies that have been around for many years. You can invest in new companies once you gain appropriate experience and profit from your initial investments—companies like Apple, Amazon, Tesla, Netflix, Disney, Microsoft, Alphabet, Visa, Starbucks, etc. There are hundreds of them; find the best ones according to what suits your investment strategy and then proceed.

7. **Dividends are vital:** If you were about to ignore dividends, stop right there! Dividends are essential, reliable income. It is an annual reward a shareholder receives as an appreciation for investing in the company. The board members usually decide what percentage of dividends are to be paid to their shareholders. So, if you want to create a consistent source of cash flow every single year, regardless of market movements, dividends are the way to go. Depending on the company, the average dividend yield

could range anywhere from 2.5% to 6%, maybe even more. This is a great way to earn regular passive income without having to lift a finger!

8. **Inherit a long-term vision:** Short-term returns are acceptable, but long-term profits are on another level. In 2010, when the company first went public, Tesla's initial stock price was $17; fast forward to 2021, and the price reached around $900. That's a remarkable increase! Moreover, the company is set to increase its profits by 50% in the upcoming years. Long-term vision always pays its dues when managed accurately.

9. **Never take a loan to invest:** When starting out, there is no concrete evidence that all your investments will give you the imagined returns. There is no need for you to borrow money from anyone, especially banks. The stock market returns could sometimes take longer than usual; taking a loan in that matter could crush you under a pile of debt. You could lose all the money you borrowed yet still need to repay the loan. Invest your own money at first, start small if need be, whatever you are comfortable losing. Of course, our aim is not to lose money, but it should be manageable if we do. There's no better quote to suit this scenario than the one by Ed Seykota, who says, *"Risk no more than you can afford to lose, and also risk enough so that a win is meaningful."*

10. **Invest regularly and continue to monitor:** Regularly investing a small amount gives you an upper hand in the stock market world. The appreciation could lead to more profit. Save a portion of your earnings, pocket money, or any other income you may receive, and allocate this to your investments each month. Do not try to get in with one large sum; that could be disastrous. Instead, invest a fixed amount of whatever you can afford, let's say every month, and keep monitoring how your stocks are performing. The stock market is highly volatile, and for that reason, do not

leave the market untouched. You don't want to return after a long time of not checking and discovering that the company you invested in has gone out of business. It is crucial that you keep tabs and strategize accordingly to keep any losses to a minimum. I check my portfolio daily; however, it would be fine to do so weekly or even monthly, but the more regular, the better.

There you have the 10 commandments, some essential rules to help you invest as a beginner. Learn them diligently and always keep them in the back of your mind, ready to be accessed whenever needed. They are titled commandments for a reason; so, do not break them, not initially anyway.

Throughout the book, you would have noticed that "research" was mentioned many times. It is the essence of the stock market. But most books only tell you to do the research; nobody actually explains HOW to research in the first place. I wanted this book to be a one-stop solution for all your investing needs as a beginner; hence, this section was a must-have.

HOW TO DO THE RESEARCH

There are two strategies you'll use to do your research in order to identify the best stocks to buy, which we'll explore:

1. Qualitative Analysis (non-numbers based), and

2. Quantitative Analysis (numbers based)

Basically, the first step focuses on non-numbers-based data such as what the company does and how it makes its money, who runs it, its growth potential, and its competitive advantage. The 2nd step, Quantitative Analysis, focuses on the facts and numbers. This is where we will look at the company's financials in detail to see how it is performing.

Tip: *A simple method to memorize the difference between each is to think of the terms 'quality,' and 'quantity.' Qualitative is to measure something by its quality, which is how we describe something, such as what the company does. Quantitative is the* *opposite, measuring by quantity, i.e., its numbers, what it earns.*

QUALITATIVE ANALYSIS (non-numbers based)

Qualitative analysis comprises five steps that we will follow to conduct the first phase of our research in determining which stocks to buy.

1. INVEST BASED ON YOUR INTERESTS

The first step is to find companies to research. One way to start your investing journey is to figure out what you are interested in. The main purpose of this task is to discover the industries and companies that you're passionate about. If you don't like a specific industry or company, you don't need to waste your time on it. You will never commit to it wholeheartedly. For instance, if you are not a big fan of the fashion industry, you will be bored researching and owning Ralph Lauren Corporation (RL) stocks.

Conversely, suppose you're investing in an industry or a company that you find interesting. In that case, there is more chance that you will conduct extensive research and keep up to date with current events surrounding that industry. Moreover, you are more likely to follow through even if the stocks' market value fluctuates, resulting in a series of slight short-term losses. This is because you will not give up on them. For instance, you will be more interested in owning Apple (AAPL) stocks if you love technology.

"The main life lesson from investing: self-interest is the most powerful force on earth, and can get people to embrace and defend almost anything." – Jesse Livermore.

Adam Mlamali, a 19-year-old UK-based teen, says that being able to invest in areas he was interested in drove him to the stock market. He was able to turn £200 ($280) into more than £200,000 ($280,000). In an interview, he said: *"For me, I was heavily interested in space really early on, only because I wanted to be an astronaut when I was younger. I was an early investor into Virgin Galactic, and Virgin Galactic was probably my best performing stock. I made over 100 percent at the end of it."*

You can analyze yourself to figure out precisely what you like and what you don't like. Getting to know what you're interested in is pretty easy; simply ask yourself the following questions:

- What do you spend your money on?
- Which technology products do you use?
- Which services do you subscribe to?
- Which brands do you use?
- What products and services are essential in your job or day-to-day life?

For example, let's say you post a video to Snapchat of you messing around while bored at your job at Walmart. Perhaps you use a Samsung phone to record the video. You may want to edit it on your Apple computer later using Adobe software before posting it to Facebook, and you are wearing Nike sneakers in the video you recorded of yourself. Without realizing it, you already have some very cool companies to start researching: Facebook, Snapchat, Samsung, Apple, Adobe, Walmart, & Nike.

Here are a few things to consider.

- **Your hobbies**: What sparks your attention in your free time? What are the one or two things you can do for the rest of your life? Do you like to draw? Do you like to scroll through social media? Do you love technology or binge-watching TV shows? Do you like playing games? Or do you have a particular liking for fast and luxurious cars? Make a list of all the things that get you going.

- **Work**: Since you are a teenager, your options may be limited. You can always find out what your friends or relatives do for a living that intrigues you, then choose stocks on that basis. Another technique is to think about what your dream job is. Who do you really want to work for? Or, who is that one business tycoon that you just can't get enough of? Which companies do they own? This will help you choose stocks based on your dreams. For instance, if you love Elon Musk as an entrepreneur, you relate to his struggles and story, as most people do, you know that you want to work for him on some level. Maybe you want to get hired in Tesla; by this, you can invest in some of the companies started by Elon Musk. You will have an emotional connection to these that you can be passionate about.

- **Products**: One of the easiest ways to know what to invest in is to look around yourself. What toys or gadgets do you play with and use? What games or products do you love? It could be Sony if you like PlayStation, Microsoft if you like Xbox, or even Baskin-Robbins if cake and ice cream is your thing! Also, the products you use daily, such as your makeup, clothing brands you wear, or sports equipment you use. Investing in the companies you love is a great first step.

- **Local Companies**: Are there any companies in your area that you feel connected to? Perhaps because they are from the same place as you, or where you have had amazing experiences, or you love what they are doing for the community? For instance, let's say you love your local coffee shop, Starbucks, which makes delicious coffee. This is where you usually meet your friends and have some great memories hanging out there; you can feel a special place for that company, can't you? So, consider investing in those as well.

2. UNDERSTAND THE BUSINESS

Now that you have selected some companies to consider, the next step is understanding their business. You need to learn about the company—what it does, how it makes its money, which products and services it offers, where it is based, and who buys its products. All this data is readily available in the company's annual report or 10-K report. I prefer the 10-K report as it is more comprehensive, so download this report for the company you are researching by searching in Google for the 'company name' and '10-K report'. In the 'Business' section of the report, you will find a description of what the business does, the products and services it offers, and how it makes its money—read through this to learn about it. In addition, there are various other sections you can read through that will help you gain a better understanding of the business and its operations. Take in as much information as possible.

One of America's most successful investors, Warren Buffett, uses the Circle of Competence method when deciding investments.

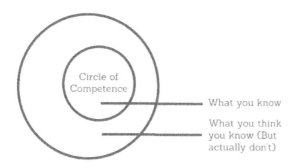

In this diagram, the small circle is an area in which you have mastered the skills you have learned through your personal experiences, giving you an advantage over others. The larger circle is the area you may have some knowledge of, but not as much as you have in the smaller circle. Abhishek Chakraborty describes it as: *"The bigger circle is what you think you know - where you are not really an expert, and the smaller circle*

inside the bigger one is what you really know - where you are an expert."

Putting this into practice, let's say you are not into sports and instead love gaming, specifically PlayStation. Your friend doesn't really play games but is obsessed with basketball, being a fan of the New York Knicks. You each have different circles of competence, yours being gaming and theirs being basketball. You both have some knowledge of each other's passions; however, you will have a more in-depth understanding of gaming than your friend, and vice versa. You would be more interested in researching and investing in the PlayStation company—Sony (SONY)—than you would in The Madison Square Garden Sports Corp. (MSGS), encompassing holdings of the Knicks.

Warren Buffett says, *"What an investor needs is the ability to correctly evaluate selected businesses. Note that word "selected": You don't have to be an expert on every company, or even many. You only have to be able to evaluate companies within your circle of competence. The size of that circle is not very important; knowing its boundaries, however, is vital."*

3. COMPETITIVE EDGE

What is a competitive edge? It is something that puts a company in an advantageous or superior business position above its competitors. This is what protects a company from its competitors. Below are some of the competitive advantages to look for when selecting a stock:

- **Switching costs** – how easy or tough is it for you to switch to a competitor. For example, if you wish to switch banks, it is quite a pain switching accounts, cards, direct debits/standing orders, etc., so you are likely to just stay with your current bank.

- **Brand power** – A good brand that is trusted by its customers. For example, Apple's brand is well known for its high-quality design and competitive prices, as is Nike, Ford, etc.

- **Barriers to entry** – What is the difficulty of a rival entering the same market? For example, transport—how many people could simply start their own network of intercity trains tomorrow? Not many! This is an industry that has a high barrier to entry because it is difficult to get into.

- **Network effects** – This is when a product or service becomes popular as more people use it. This adds value as more people want it because others have it. For instance, Facebook and Instagram are only popular because everyone else is on it too.

- **Economies of scale** – These are cost advantages that companies benefit from by making production more efficient. Larger companies can produce more products at a lower cost. They can buy in bulk at lower prices and charge customers less because they can supply their products for less. Small companies have to charge more for their products because buying or producing their goods is more expensive. Because of their size, companies such as Amazon and Walmart enjoy massive economies of scale.

- **Intellectual property** or **trade secrets** - Do you know the Coca-Cola or Kentucky Fried Chicken recipe? Nobody else does, so other companies cannot replicate this. This gives them a competitive advantage.

- **Pricing power** – This is the effect that changing the price of a product or service has on the demand of that product or service, i.e., how likely the customer is still going to buy it at the new price. For example, if a company has weak pricing power, a price increase will reduce customers' demand because they will probably choose an alternative—a cheaper product. But a company with strong pricing power usually provides a unique product with low competition. So, if they increased their price, the demand from customers probably wouldn't change because there is no alternative product for the customer to choose instead. For example, if Netflix or Spotify increases their price by $1-$2 tomorrow, you would probably pay it as there aren't many other competitors offering the same quality service. Apple is another example; when they released the first iPhone, they had strong pricing power because it was the only smartphone with associated apps at the time. As a result, they could charge a higher price, but their pricing power was reduced when other companies introduced similar competitive products.

4. COMPANY MANAGEMENT

In any good sports team, you need a good captain to lead the team to a win. A company is no different; its leadership decides the direction and focus of its operations and how fast it grows.

The company's leader most likely has their salary and benefits tied to the company's performance. So, they are motivated to ensure the company performs well. Therefore, in your research, you will want to find out the following:

- Does the company have a founding CEO, i.e., did that person help start the company, or were they employed later on?

- What is your impression of the CEO?

- What's the CEO's rating on Glassdoor.com?

- What percentage of the company do insiders own?

What we want to see in our research when it comes to leadership is:

- A founder-led company, or if not founder-led, then someone who is very invested in the company or has a lot of experience in relevant industries.

- A CEO that is popular with their employees. You can find a CEO's rating on Glassdoor.com by searching the company name and looking at their rating. Anything over 80% is considered pretty good.

- A good level of insider ownership – 5% or more. Insiders are usually the founders and employees of the company that owns more than 10% of the voting shares. You can find the percentage of insider ownership on Yahoo Finance. Simply locate the company, go to the 'Statistics' tab. Under the 'Share Statistics' heading, it shows the percentage held by insiders. We like to see higher than 5%. The higher this percentage, the better because this means there is more incentive for the employees to grow the company.

5. GROWTH ABILITY

Now, we need to understand what the future potential is for the growth of the company. We want to find companies that will be around for the long term, advance, and grow. To assist with this, ask yourself the following questions:

- Is the business operating in a fast or slow-growing industry?

- Do you think the company's products and services will still be relevant over the long term in the next 5 to 20 years?

- How does the firm fare against its rivals? Is it able to stand out from the crowd?

- What do customers think of the products or services the company offers?

What we are looking for by asking these questions is to find companies who:

- Are in fast-growing, future-relevant industries. An example may be the green energy industry. This will probably replace the gas & oil industries in the future. Electric cars could be another industry of the future that will replace petrol cars.

- Have a strong, loyal customer base that loves their products or services. For example, think about all those passionate customers obsessed with Apple products. They will queue for hours to buy the latest releases and probably own the whole range, including iPhone, iPad, Macbook, and Airpods. They will refuse to buy any other brands as they love the Apple brand.

- Offer a unique or competitive product or service. For example, Apple's iPhone has consistently remained the best-selling smartphone. This is primarily due to its unique user-friendly iOS interface, which many companies have tried somewhat unsuccessfully to replicate.

SUMMARY

Find great stocks using Qualitative Analysis by:

- Looking where you spend your money already.

- Investing in companies you understand.

- Finding companies that have competitive advantages.

- Finding the companies with strong leadership.

- Looking at growing industries.

QUANTITATIVE ANALYSIS (numbers based)

Now that you have finished phase 1 of your research, having found companies of interest, and learned about their business, we can begin phase 2 and dive into their numbers. From the annual report or 10-K report you downloaded earlier, you could analyze the company's performance and financials. In this section, however, we will use Yahoo Finance because all the info we need is available for multiple companies in one place, making the comparison of companies easier. During the analysis, you may be overwhelmed at first sight of all the data, so if you feel overwhelmed, do not worry. We will take it step-by-step, making it easy to understand and follow. Just trust the process. We will concentrate our analysis on the key financial figures to determine if the stock is a good buy.

Locate the companies you want to research on Yahoo Finance, and let's begin.

1. Note the **current share price** (the number below the company name). The share price isn't a good indicator of a company's value; it doesn't contribute much to your analysis, but you need to know how much a share costs to buy it.

2. Check the chart to see the **trend in the share price** for the periods one year, five years, and max - ideally, you want to see a steady increase in the pattern over the long term.

3. Check its **Market Cap** – This is the overall market value of the company at the time. Why is Market Cap important? It can be used as a point of reference to indicate the company's

relative size for you to compare against other company sizes. For example, a company with a Market Cap of $50 billion is much larger in size than one which is $1 billion, and it could give you an idea of how much room the company has to grow relative to its competitors. So, the $1B company could potentially grow to a $50B company.

4. **P/E Ratio** – For now, all you need to know about this is that if there is a number in this section, then that means the company is profitable. If there is no number under the P/E ratio, that means it is currently not profitable. P/E ratio is typically used to indicate if a stock is cheap or expensive. It reveals how much investors are ready to pay for a dollar of profit. The greater the ratio, the more eager investors are to invest. If this number is very high, it could either be that it is overvalued and expensive, or it could be that investors are seeing a lot of future growth potential for the company and are pricing that growth into the ratio.

Tip: *When comparing companies, the P/E ratio is usually only useful when comparing companies in the same industry, e.g., Nike vs. Adidas instead of Nike vs. Apple. One is Apparel & Sports, and the other is Technology, so they are very different.*

5. **Debt & Cash** - On the 'Statistics' tab: Focus on **market cap** and **enterprise value** to understand debt and cash.

- If the market cap figure is higher than the enterprise value, the company has more cash than debt

- The opposite is true; if enterprise value is higher than market cap, that means the company has more debt than cash

For long-term investing, we like to see companies with more cash than debt (a strong cash balance). However, this should not be the make or break in your decision if it has more debt, but understand that having more cash than debt means the company has more money for expansion and growth, which is what we want to see.

6. On the **'Financials'** tab: What we want to focus on here are the following lines:

- **Total Revenue**
- **Cost of Revenue**
- **Gross Profit**

These charts show the annual financials for each year/period and are read from the right (oldest) to the left (newest). The TTM column stands for Trailing Twelve Month average, which is for the previous 12 months.

All we want to see here is **Total Revenue increasing** and **Gross Profits increasing**:

- **Total Revenue** is increasing year on year.

- **Cost of Revenue** – This is what they need to spend to generate this Total Revenue. It could be raw materials, salaries, etc.

- **Gross Profit** – This is the company's profit after deducting the costs associated with making and selling its products or services. The gross profit in these columns is the Total Revenue minus the Cost of Revenue. What we want to see here is that the Gross Profit increases over time. Don't worry too much if one of these years, it went slightly down; the main thing is that overall, it is increasing.

Some other metrics to consider:

- **Gross Margin** – This is the percentage of revenue that exceeds a company's costs of goods sold. You may hear people referring to Gross Margin widening or narrowing. Margins widening is good. Basically, it means you are making more profit, and it is costing you less to produce goods and services to generate those profits. The less it costs, the more money you make. A company wants to have the highest margins possible, so it costs them less money to make more profit. You can locate a company's gross margins on Morningstar.com. On the company's page, click 'Key Ratios,' then 'Full Key Ratios Data,' which will take you to a page showing the **Gross Margin %** for each year. As a rough guide for the level of gross margins you want to see:

- 0% - 30% = Risky

- 30% - 50% = Acceptable

- 50% or more = Fantastic!

- **Net income** - This is known as the 'Bottom Line.' Net income is the profit you can take home after all your expenses. You can think of Net Income as a fisherman catching fish in his net that he gets to bring home. It is defined as the amount of revenue left after subtracting all expenses, taxes, and costs. Our goal with net income is to see that the earnings rise along with its revenues, i.e., the net income and total revenue increase. Just because a company's revenue increases doesn't mean its net income increases. We just want to see when looking at this that both increase simultaneously.

7. **Check what the analysts are saying** – Under the 'Analysis' tab.

- **How many analysts** are covering the stock that provides their estimates on it? This is just an indicator of how many analysts are covering it and the level of interest in the company. This can be anywhere from 0 - 30 or even 40 - 50 analysts covering a stock (for the larger companies, it is usually on the higher end, and for smaller companies, on the lower end).

- **Revenue Estimate** – Check the **Avg. Estimate** line – what is the expected revenue growth target for this year and next year? There is a **Sales Growth** percentage line at the bottom which shows the estimated growth in percentage. This demonstrates how much the company may grow its sales; the higher the number, the better. What is a good sales growth rate? As a very rough estimate, anything over 20%-25% is usually pretty good, but bear in mind this can vary from industry to industry, company size, and how long the company has been operating. Smaller or fast-growing companies would usually have a much higher growth rate than a company that has been around for a long time.

- **Earnings Estimate** – Check the **Avg. Estimate** line. This is an analyst's estimated forecast for a company's future **earnings per share (EPS)**. It is used in determining a company's fair value. Whenever a company misses, beats, or meets its earnings estimate, it can impact the stock price, so companies try to meet or beat the earnings estimates. Companies tend to manage their earnings carefully as a result. Generally, companies that consistently beat earnings estimates usually outperform the market and vice versa. What we are looking for in this metric is to ideally see an increase in the current Avg. Estimate from this year to next year. So, if the current EPS of a stock is 0.10 and the following year is 0.20, the earnings per share are expected to double, which is a good sign, showing high growth. You can also look at this value as a percentage figure which can be easier to understand. Under the heading 'Growth Estimates,' the percentage growth for the next year will be shown as a percentage value demonstrating its growth over the next year.

8. Determine the **Fair Value of the stock**.

- With fair value, I mean the current value of the stock in the market. What value is it trading for (share price), and is it beneficial to buyers and sellers? You can easily calculate if the current price is fair by determining the value of the business. You will recall the term 'Market Capitalization' or 'Market Cap' for short–this is the company's value. Under the 'Statistics' tab on Yahoo Finance, locate the number of 'Shares outstanding;' this is the number of shares available. Simply divide the total value of the business (market cap) by the number of shares available (shares outstanding). You will get the value per share. For example, if the market cap is $50 billion and the shares outstanding is 4 billion, then 50 divided by 4 is $12.50; this price is its fair value.

- Now, if the value per share comes to $12.50 as above, and you notice it is trading for less than this on the open market, say $11.05, then it is a fair price as there is a good chance the price will go back up to its original $12.50. On the other hand, if it is trading higher than $12.50, say $18.99, it may be overpriced and not a good time to buy. It would be wise to start buying shares when they are lower than the fair value. However, pull up the stock chart and find out at which point of the month or year the stock price fell and then try to figure out the reason behind it falling. The cause of big drops or rises could be your clue.

- Make an excel sheet to keep all your records in one place and look at them whenever you feel the need. Finally, when you're ready, you should wait for the exact buying opportunity. It may sound hypothetical, but it works. You should never purchase a stock that is declining because you never know how much lower it may fall. For example, you might think that $11.05 is pretty low compared to its original price of $12.50, but hold on. If you buy, and the price continues to go down, you miss an opportunity to buy at a lower price. It might go to $10 or even less. That is why you should buy stocks only when the share price has touched the bottom and is now rising a little. That's when you could gain the most profit out of it.

There you have it, a simple and effective way to help you conduct your research and decide your investments. It will hopefully be very beneficial to you. Remember, if you want a complete list of websites and free resources you can use to help with your research, check out www.jp-clarke.com/resources.

Let's review everything we learned in this chapter before moving on to organizing your strategies in the following chapter.

SUMMARY

Find great stocks using Quantitative Analysis by:

- Checking the current share price.

- Checking the chart to see the share price trend showing a steady increase over the long term.

- Check its market cap to understand the size of the company.

- Check the P/E ratio to identify if the company is profitable or not. Remember, if there is a number, it is profitable, and if there is no number or shows N/A, then it isn't. P/E ratio could be used later to assess whether a stock is cheap or expensive as you gain more experience.

- Check if the company has more cash than debt by using the market cap and enterprise values. If the market cap figure is higher than the enterprise value, the company has more cash than debt and vice versa.

- Check that the annual financials for each year/period show an increase in Total Revenue and Gross Profits year on year.

- Check the company's Gross Margin % on Morningstar.com:

- 0% - 30% = Risky

- 30% - 50% = Acceptable

- 50% or more = Fantastic!

- Check that the Net Income AND Total Revenue increases simultaneously.

- Check what the analysts are saying.

  o How many analysts are covering the stock?

  o Revenue Estimate – Check the Avg. Estimate for Revenue growth increases for this year and the following year. To see this figure as a percentage, check the Sales Growth estimate line; 20% and above is usually a reasonable rough estimate for sales growth, but remember that this depends on various factors.

  o Earnings Estimate – Check the Avg. Estimate forecast for a company's future earnings per share (EPS); we want to see it increase from this year to next year.

- Determine the fair value of the stock by dividing the market cap by the number of shares available. Then compare this figure against the current share price to help determine if you are getting a good deal. If the current share price is below fair value, it could be an excellent time to buy.

- Make an excel sheet to record your research.

- When deciding when to buy if the share price is going down, wait for the price to go down and then buy as soon as you see it start to increase so you can try to buy at its bottom price.

CHAPTER 6

STEP 5

STRATEGIZE AND ORGANIZE

"Strategy without tactics is the slowest route to victory. Tactics without strategy is the noise before defeat."

– Sun Tzu

The fifth step towards a life of fulfillment is hidden behind the curtain of strategy and organization. No two forces could be as powerful as creating a strategy and then organizing it for maximum results. In this chapter, you will learn the real reason why investors and traders are so fixated upon strategizing their plan of action and how to create one for yourself. Furthermore, discover the kind of organization teens can implement when investing in stocks. If you look up the word "strategy," you will understand that it means creating a master plan of action intended to achieve a long-term goal. The stock market is filled with uncertainty; you need to have a solid strategy up your sleeve to provide some order and inspiration for a definitive victory.

At just 16, Justin Brosseau put his life savings, only $650, into three stocks: Citi (C), GE (GE), and United Airlines (UAL). He made nearly 250% return on his investments before graduating from Miami University. While his friends were wasting their money going out and having a good time, Justin strategized and formulated his next move to profit from his investments. At the time, he made about $1600 on his investments, whereas his friends relied on pocket money from their parents. People like Justin are successful because they are smart enough to formulate an investment plan and stick to it. Justin, now 23, says, *"I enjoy taking risks; I'll never stop investing. There's always a way to win. I just want to be that person to figure it out."*

WHY SHOULD YOU STRATEGIZE?

Once you've decided on a concrete goal that satisfies your needs and makes you happy, it is only logical that you find ways to achieve that goal. Of course, there is more than one way to reach it. You will be wise to find the best route that takes you there in the shortest time possible with minimal obstacles along the way. I mean, for instance, if I give you a treasure map for a chest filled with gold and tell you to start your journey in finding that chest, what will you do? You will snatch the map and start looking for the quickest and easiest way to get to the gold!

You look at the map and assess all the available routes and risks each pose, as well as the time it will take you to get there. One may be a plain, safe, and boring route that will take you six months to reach the chest. While it is the safest option, it will take ages to get the gold. The second route may take you there in only one month but is extremely high risk with life-threatening obstacles that could cause severe physical and mental harm. The third route will take you there in just two months. While it has obstacles that you know you can overcome, there are some exciting landscapes and sights to explore and experience along the way. Which of these three would you choose? I assume you've selected the third one; it involves fewer risks and takes you to your chest in good time.

In this example, what you did was essentially assess the risks, formulate a strategy, map out your route, and manage the obstacles along the way. You would have devised a plan to get there quickly. At the same time, you enjoy the journey, beat the minor obstacles along the way, and eventually be the owner of the greatest treasure ever buried—pretty sleek, isn't it!? The key is to analyze all the routes you can take to achieve your goal, choose the best one, and then map out your road to success.

It is precisely what you will be doing in your journey towards finding the treasure of financial independence. Jim Rohn said, "*Success is 20% skills and 80% strategy. You might know how to succeed, but more importantly, what's your plan to succeed?*" Creating a rigid strategy will help you keep your head in the game and focus on the goal. Moreover, you can organize your investments and make consecutive changes to plan your next moves. Strategies work best when you know what you're doing. Here are a few benefits of having a strategy in place:

- **A clear sense of direction:** You cannot get anywhere if you don't know where you're headed. When you've formulated an actionable plan leading to one specific outcome, you avoid distraction and increase follow through.

- **Highly proactive:** With your buying and selling regime, a strategy ensures you can be proactive at any given time. Having a strategy in place enables you to foresee and predict the economy's future, perhaps the stock movements. If you predict unfavorable and uncertain situations in advance, you can immediately create a plan to tackle them beforehand. You don't have to be reactive, only acting after the conditions have arrived. You can act beforehand based on your researched predictions. Let's have a look at COVID-19, for example. Suppose you were able to acknowledge, in the early stages, the worldwide impact it would have on shutting down various industries.

In that case, you could have predicted a shift in the markets and developed a strategy where you would buy stocks at a discount due to the dip in their prices, investing in industries that would showcase the promise of increased growth based on how the virus would change the way we do things on a daily basis. Examples include home delivery food services like Uber Eats or Amazon Pantry or binge-watching services like Netflix, Prime, and Hulu. Not to mention platforms that would make working from home or attending classes easier, such as Zoom. These were great companies to invest in that could have been purchased at huge discounts and have since increased in value. With such a strategy and the ability to take action and adapt quickly, you could have made tremendous profits. That's called being proactive. "A strategy is necessary because the future is unpredictable." – Robert Waterman.

- **Less procrastination and negativity:** It's easy to get distracted in a world of plenty, with so many investments to choose from. Once you've decided what you want and created a clear strategy that you stick to, there is no room left for procrastination or confusion. You now know exactly what to do to achieve your goal, and the rest is just noise.

- **Efficient and optimized journey:** Your strategy will include the most efficient way to reach your goals by achieving maximum productivity with minimum effort, time, or expense. Referring to the example of the treasure map I mentioned earlier, choosing the third route is the most efficient way to reach the treasure. This is because the first was the longest, and the second was the most dangerous.

- **Holds you accountable**: Strategy will let you build realistic checkpoints or milestones, making it easier to achieve your goals and measure your progress. For example, let's assume you set a goal of owning 12 profitable stocks within one year. You can set milestones breaking your target into bite-sized chunks. This could be twelve milestones of buying one stock every month, or you could do four milestones buying three stocks every three months. This way, you have smaller, more realistic steps to achieve. If you don't reach the first milestone, you can assess why not and hold yourself accountable; readjust accordingly and work your way to finally own the targeted stocks in the set timeframe.

- **Strength and weakness:** It's crucial to analyze yourself to leverage your strengths and mitigate weaknesses. For example, if you know that you can work better with short breaks in-between, that's your strength. On the other hand, once you take a long break and get too comfortable, it becomes your weakness. Perhaps you are more analytically inclined and love numbers; this is a strength for stock analysis. Conversely, if you don't like numbers, this may be your weakness, and you then know you need to work on this more or find ways to make it more enjoyable.

- **Right stock mix:** Your strategy will include detailing which stocks you should buy and sell. Some stocks provide regular dividend income, so these would be a good choice if your goal is to generate steady cash flow. Others offer long-term gains with no dividends, so they are better suited if you are happy to only take profits when you sell them later on. Owning the right combination of long-term profitable stocks with a little bit of short-term risk is worth it. Strategizing will tell you which ones you should set your sights on.

- **Solidifies the purpose:** There is a 90% chance that you may give up on your plan at some point. But once you have the strategy to achieve your goal, a clear and attainable one, your purpose will be more within reach. Strategy solidifies vision. American academic Michael Porter said, *"Sound strategy starts with having the right goal."*

- **Framework for success:** The most fantastic benefit of having a strategy is that it creates an outline under which you can make all the decisions you need to achieve your end goal. It creates a framework, which you can utilize to follow as a schedule. It also makes it easy to get back on track if you become distracted.

- **Reduces wasteful activities:** A clear route with a definite goal usher you away from wasteful activities. You will not commit to things that will destroy your productivity or consume too much of your time. You can do only a few things in a day and still be super productive. In contrast, the opposite is true, you can do a million things in a day, but if they don't align with your end goal, you have just wasted your time and nothing else.

Brett Sifling was a typical 14-year-old teen who was always on his computer playing games, messing around on social media, and even doing a bit of coding. Until one day, his teacher showed him an account invested profitably in Apple (AAPL) stock. This is when he found the stock market and began trading. Like most successful investors, Brett devised a strategy and set achievable goals and milestones. One personal goal was to earn enough to travel to New York, the financial capital of the world, as well as Vegas and Europe. He made $15,000 on a single biotech stock trade before he was even old enough to get a driver's license! Setting and achieving goals allowed him to travel. He met highly successful people, spent time with them, and learned as much as possible. It is these experiences that establish a significant foundation for a better future.

STRATEGIES FOR INVESTING

After understanding the importance of strategizing, it is only logical to create a clear strategy for yourself. However, before you start strategizing a plan based on your individual goals, I would like to give you a few common strategies that you can incorporate within your investment plan.

1. **Growth Investing**: Don't get overwhelmed; growth investing is pretty simple. The idea is that the company will grow and eventually result in higher stock prices, resulting in higher profits for you. It is a strategy that most beginners use to get into the stock market game. The strategy is to look for; you guessed it—growth! Look for momentum. This means checking out companies climbing in price, increasing their net value, and having some serious momentum and support to continue the trend. With growth companies, the share price may be high compared to their earnings, and you may not earn dividends when they are in their growth phase, but they are worth investing in as the growth is mostly planned out and inevitable if everything goes right for them.

   Your mission is to find and invest in such companies. You must keep track of the growth stocks you invest in as there may be a time when the growth slows down and their value decreases; you should try to predict the company's future based on your research and be ready if that time comes. For example, Apple has shown tremendous growth over the years, having traded at around $0.10 at one point, eventually reaching a high of approximately $150.

Imagine buying $1000 of Apple's stock at $0.10 and selling at $150, making $1.5m! Growth stocks are growing a lot faster than the regular stocks in the market; finding and investing in them is a risk-reward factor. With time, it could make you rich. They generate earnings at a rapid speed. As a growth investor, your eyes are always on the next big thing, the next upcoming long-term trend that people might adopt and stick to for a long time. You don't just become a growth investor; you must do some serious research before investing in any company that provides little to no return in the first few months or even years.

There are a few characteristics of growth stocks that will help you identify them. The first is the most obvious one; the stock will have a very high growth rate in terms of earnings and performance compared to other companies in similar industries. For example, let's assume the company you are researching has earnings growth of 20% every year for three years or more, and competitors in the same industry have an average growth rate over the same period of 10%; this can be seen as a growth stock as it is growing at double the rate of its competitors.

The second characteristic of a growth stock is a very low or no dividend payout. If a company is not paying any dividend to its shareholders, it could mean that it is developing so fast that instead of paying dividends, they invest their capital into growing the company. As a result, they will earn their profits and reinvest them back into the business to continue growing. That, in fact, boosts their ability to generate higher revenue.

The third characteristic could be the advantage they possess over their competition. You noticed that they have a higher growth rate; why do you think that is? It is because they have something their competitors don't or are doing something better. Google became a giant monopoly because there was no one as qualified and as dedicated in the market. There were competitors like Yahoo and Bing, but eventually, Google outclassed them all as they found a way to make their platform better than their competitors. That's a growth investment. Growth stocks have a sense of competitive advantage in a similar industry. This edge enables them to sell their products and grow faster; it's their unique selling proposition (USP).

The fourth attribute to finding growth companies is that they have a loyal customer fan base. People love their products and don't mind waiting in a queue for hours to get their hands on their latest launches. It is astonishing to witness such loyalty among fans for a particular company. It is proof that they are doing a fantastic job in narrating their brand story, attracting people to try their products, and paying a premium to own some of their line-ups. I know the name of a company is popping into your mind while reading this paragraph. That's right; you are already becoming able to recognize them!

The fifth attribute of a growth company is the substantial amount of revenue they generate. There is no dividend and no short-term gain. Instead, people who hold the stock over the long term usually witness a growth of not 200% or 300%, but much larger multiples, and are super happy with themselves for investing in the early growth phase.

The final trait is the risk factor. You didn't think that such tremendous profit would just land on your laps for nothing, did you? So, there is always a fair chance that you might lose all the money you invested over the years. Now, that's heartbreaking, but the people who commit to proper research and are open to playing against the odds may be rewarded handsomely. Some famous examples of such growth companies include Amazon, Apple, Tesla, and Netflix. That's correct, the giants that are paramount to the industry. But bear in mind, not all growth stocks are large conglomerates; they are often smaller startup companies. Startups tend to grow a lot faster than established companies, but there is also more risk of failing. According to the U.S. Bureau of Labor Statistics, approximately 20% of new businesses fail during their first two years of trading, and 45% fail within the first five years. Only 25% of new businesses actually make it to fifteen years or more. Using the research method you learned in the previous chapter, your job is to find the growth companies that will make it to 15 years or more. Maybe you can find the next 'Apple' scenario and make $1.5m in profit!

2. **Value Investing**: It basically means checking out the value and true worth of the stock before investing in it. You are trying to find stocks that are believed to be worth more than the price they are selling for; they are essentially undervalued. You are bargain hunting! I think you will agree that when buying the latest iPhone, whether on sale at a discount or full price, you are still getting the same iPhone with the same features, just at different prices. Stocks are similar in that their share price can change even if the company value has remained constant. Buying them on sale gives you more value; value investing is finding these secret sales. Brokers use this strategy to make money in the short term. When the price of specific stocks goes down for some reason, or they find stocks that nobody is looking at and are undervalued, they buy and wait for the price to increase, then sell for a profit.

Finding such stocks that are underappreciated or undervalued is the key here. When you predict that the company will go up quickly, you buy and hold such stocks in bulk and later sell them to make an attractive profit. The clue here is in your research; by determining if the stock is undervalued. Charlie Munger once said, *"All intelligent investing is value investing – acquiring more than you are paying for."*

3. **Diversification**: This is the strategy you already know a lot about, as discussed in the fourth chapter. In essence, to avoid any massive loss, investors scatter their funds across the stock market and purchase stocks from various companies, industries, countries, etc. The more their diversification, the lower their risk, which usually also means slightly less profit. The less diversified they are, the more profit, and inevitably, more risk as well. Risk and profit are directly connected with one other; the key is to find a balance between the two that aligns with your personal goals.

YOUR FIRST INVESTMENT STRATEGY

With the basics covered, you are now ready to create your own investment strategy; how exciting! Of course, your first investment strategy is essential because nobody wants to suffer failure on the first attempt. Do not get discouraged, though; you have time by your side, and of course, ME to help and guide you along the way. You can download some awesome goal-setting tools for free at www.jp-clarke.com/resources. Your plan starts with the most important factor of all:

- **The Result**: Before you can start setting goals, you first need to identify the result, or outcome, that you want to reach through your goals. The difference between the result and your goals is that the result is the end game of what you want to achieve, for instance, to be financially free. Your goals are the steps you will take to achieve the result. I'm guessing the reason you even picked up this book is to become financially free, but how do we do this? Robert Kiyosaki, the author of *Rich Dad Poor Dad*, says, *"The only way to become financially independent is to accumulate income-generating assets which can pay for your expenses."* The income-generating assets, in our case, will be the stocks we trade and earn dividends on. All you now need to do is list down all the monthly expenses you need to pay out to survive, such as rent, utilities, transport, food, entertainment, etc. If you are still living with your parents and don't have all of these just yet, you can start by covering your current expenses or usual spending money, or you can research these to find out what you would need to pay if you moved out and fended for yourself. Ask your parents what they spend. Once you have the total monthly figure, let's say it's $1500 per month as an example. You now know what monthly amount you need to earn through trading stocks to be financially free, which you can then use to figure out the next step—your goals. Your job is to create enough monthly passive income through trading stocks and earning dividends to cover this figure; at that point, you will be financially free. Simple, right?

- **Your Goal**: You cannot hit a target without seeing it. I cannot emphasize adequately the value of setting realistic goals that could change your life, one milestone at a time to keep you moving forward. Do not set some fantasy goal of making $100,000 in one month—that's ridiculous. Instead, your research will guide you through the actual returns, and based on that, you can set a goal that is achievable yet aggressive at the same time. Your goals can vary considerably and change over time; that is okay; simply update them as you progress. You can set financial and personal development goals. Your goals should be about the process, not about the results. Try not to set goals about making money, such as earning $10,000 a month, which is very hard to define and measure—this is a result, not a process. You will likely not achieve it, thereby demotivating you. Your goals should help you make money, but to make money should not be a goal you write down. Instead, you want to list goals that are the steps within the process you need to take to make money. For example, researching one company each week, finding one dividend stock a week that pays an 8% return, reading one investment book each month, attending a course or seminar, investing a portion of your income each month into stocks, or finding a stock you can trade for a 10% gain, etc. Using the $1500 per month expenditure example, you could break down your goals into achievable milestones. If you invested $5000 into a dividend stock earning 8% per year, this would be around $34 per month in earnings; it would take 44 of these stocks to generate $1500 per month in dividends. Your goals could then be set to purchase 44 of these stocks over a set period. You could also set goals based on capital gains, generating larger profits on trading stocks, building capital to help buy dividend stocks quicker. For instance, finding a stock that you can invest $5000 into, which will generate a 20% gain when selling, making $1000 that you can put into dividend stocks, and then repeating the process. You can set long-term and short-term goals; the latter are just examples, and the numbers can be adjusted to whichever levels work for you. The Australian Investors Association developed a great format to help set goals; they call it the SMART format:

Specific – each goal should be very clear and specific

Measurable – frame the goal with a measurable unit

Achievable – the goal should be realistically achievable

Relevant – needs to be relevant to the desired outcome

Time-based – assign a timeframe to track progress

Now, make a list of your goals, being as specific as possible. Then, check on them regularly to measure your progress and adjust them as needed should things change in the future.

- **Establish the boundaries of risk**: Some people have high-risk tolerance while some have low. It is not to be ashamed of; know your limit and stay within it to not break your spirit. The riskier it is, the higher the returns usually are but do not risk it all if you can't handle a negative outcome. There will be many bad decisions, but you could forge ahead towards success if you play your cards right. I would suggest that, as a beginner, you adopt a low-risk strategy to start. You will likely make mistakes along the way, so keep it low risk until you have more experience. Do not invest any money you cannot afford to lose. Start off using a demo trading account before you invest real money.

- **Decide on which investment strategies to use**: You learned about this in chapter three's primary investment strategies. Decide if you want to use Growth Investing, Value Investing, Diversification, or a combination of them. You may want to first master one strategy before moving on to the next. Perhaps you want to try them simultaneously; this is entirely up to you—my suggestion is to focus on one before moving on to the next.

- **Conduct a thorough analysis of your stocks**: You know the amount of risk you're able to handle; based on that, find stocks that are both a little riskier and less risky and group them for diversification; sort of mix-match them and then identify which ones will help you get closer to the objectives you defined in step one. For example, new companies are riskier as they are purely focused on growth; established companies are usually less risky as we all know they have been around for decades and are doing pretty well.

- **Get on and buy stocks**: You know which ones are good and which ones aren't based on your research, so what are you waiting for? Go ahead, buy the stock you want, and follow along. Trust in your research. Never be afraid to take action; start small and take the plunge!

- **Learn throughout the process**: It is normal to suffer failure and success at any point in your journey. Learn from both outcomes. The key here is consistency and a long-term vision. Nothing can throw you off track if you have done your research and played the game with a set strategy. Remember, it's not gambling; do not wish it, confirm the outcome, and predict the future.

Incredibly, you have now created your first strategy to commit yourself to the stock market. How awesome is that! Let's review everything we learned in this chapter before moving on to the next, where I'll warn you about some common mistakes you could make and how to avoid them in order to avoid losing money.

SUMMARY

1. Decide on a concrete result or outcome that you want to achieve which satisfies and makes you happy.

2. Create a definitive strategy using specific and measurable goals to achieve that result.

3. Always create a strategy that will quickly take you to your goal with the least amount of risk, especially for beginners.

4. Benefits of having a strategy in place:

   o A clear sense of direction

   o Highly proactive

   o Less procrastination and negativity

   o Efficient and optimized journey

   o Holds you accountable

   o Strength and weakness

   o Right stock mix

   o Solidifies the purpose

   o Framework for success

   o Reduces wasteful activities

5. Here are some strategies to get you started:

   o Growth Investing

   o Value Investing

   o Diversification

6. Create your first investment plan and execute it immediately to monitor the results and then readjust until you gain profits.

CHAPTER 7

STEP 6

DODGING THE MISTAKES

> *"When you make a mistake, there are only three things you should ever do about it: admit it, learn from it, and don't repeat it."*
>
> **– Paul Bear Bryant**

Wise men are those who learn from other people's mistakes. I am sure you've heard this before, and it's the ultimate truth. Few people learn from other people's mistakes, and even fewer learn from their own. It is only natural to get it wrong sometimes, and it's okay. Nobody will learn anything if they are perfect. Go ahead, make a billion mistakes, don't be concerned, just do yourself a favor, and don't make the same mistake twice. That's the key here. Once you know what the error is, it should forever stay in your mind as a lesson learned, which you can apply and teach to others. This chapter highlights the pitfalls and errors that may occur during your journey through the world of stocks.

Investor George Soros said, *"Once we realize that imperfect understanding is the human condition, there is no shame in being wrong; only in failing to correct our mistakes."*

Be wise to learn from the mistakes listed below so when the time comes, you can avoid them. Here are a few that could save you a fortune in regret.

1. **Getting emotional:** When you narrow down the cause of wild market fluctuations, you will notice that it often results from emotions. Only a small percentage of people succeed in the stock market because the rest let their emotions get the best of them. Sometimes, we can lose our self-control after we lose a little money. It's essential to keep a level head when you're investing. Any mishap is bound to cause frustration, but it's okay to go through these sentiments as a teen. The important thing is to understand that you can always turn things around if you stay calm. Loss, panic, and decision are not the best trio out there when used in combination. They drive actions that you wouldn't consider on a typical day.

I get it; reacting emotionally, getting heated, and panicking when you see your investments take a tumble is a common phenomenon. But, reacting negatively by doing something that will only make matters worse is not that smart either. You may do things such as panic-sell when your stocks dive or buying in when stocks are at their highest due to FOMO (the fear of missing out).

Don't touch your account or make rash decisions if you're in panic mode or are emotionally charged due to something happening in the market. Instead, take a step back, relax, and reassess. The most powerful emotions that force you to take hostile actions are greed and fear. When an investor is consumed by greed during the best of times and devoured by fear during the worst, they are no longer an investor. They become a stubborn kid who just doesn't listen to reason regardless of what they have learned or their research points to. So, instead, you should be doing the opposite. You should be greedy by buying loads of stocks when the market is at its lowest and fearful when the market is on the top of its game, as what goes up may often also go down at some point. The best thing to do is set your emotions aside and make rational decisions to bring you back to your normal state—decisions based on your technical analysis and research rather than emotions.

Denial isn't healthy for an investor; it is necessary that you accept the circumstance you are faced with and then plan to get out of it calmly and systematically. Sitting around in denial will only make things worse for you. This could occur when you've invested most of your money in one place, and when the company value drops, you just can't believe that you've been inflicted with such a massive loss. The bubble of euphoria in which you were previously living bursts, and the fog lifts—thus giving rise to emotional outbursts and despair—always take a more sensible outlook.

Our emotions are triggered during an investment when we develop an illogical attachment of fondness to our holdings or stocks. Invest in the company you wish to own but do not fall in love with it. It's tricky to master; excitement is a great emotion to exercise, but having too much attachment can be detrimental to your decision-making process. Remember when we discussed investing in companies you are interested in? You might be deeply connected to this company because of some childhood memory or an overwhelming appreciation and support for their products or services. Even if the company starts losing money and your research flashes warning signs to sell, you may still be hesitant to sell because you love the company so much. Avoid this at all costs—having a false attachment to things could lead to suffering and failure.

Fear of missing out or losing everything is another catalyst that ignites emotions. When you find a particular stock that everybody is talking about, you should be cautious, not excited. Research that company and only then decide. Buying stocks only because people are talking about them is not a strategy. In fact, it might go against your previously placed strategy and ruin the game.

2. **Following recommendations**: It is extremely wise to have someone by your side as a mentor who helps and guides you towards your goal. You should listen to people walking the same path as you are, but who are more experienced or just ahead of you, but that doesn't mean that you will follow it as an absolute word of God. You should be careful of who you take advice from. For example, some people may influence you to invest in certain companies because their friend, who by the way has never bought a stock in their life, said "they heard it's the next big thing" or "they predicted enormous growth." Avoid such speculation which is not factual. You will risk your portfolio by following the advice you're not entirely sure of; stick to what you know and love. I'm not suggesting that you fully disregard them, but instead to ensure you do your own research.

Follow your own instincts and research, not the word-of-mouth coming from someone else. Deciding to invest in a stock based on what your best friend heard, or thinks they know, is not a good enough reason to actually invest in it. It could provide some great options for you to explore; however, you need to carry out your own study to see if it's a decent investment. You should only make that investment when the company fits your strategy and aligns with your goals and principles. Oprah Winfrey said, *"Follow your instincts. That's where true wisdom manifests itself."*

3. **Investing with a trader's mindset:** It's vital that when you invest, you do not do so with a day trader's mentality. The difference is between short and long-term mentality. Making a quick buck is not the goal; the reason you're invested in stocks is to build a life of freedom. Making $10 a day by buying and selling stocks means nothing if you can earn $1000 simply by holding them. Having a long-term perspective will be your greatest skill as an investor— think in terms of years, not days, weeks, or months. There are thousands of examples where investors lost money because they sold their shares too early and ran for the exit. Holding them instead would actually have resulted in higher gains. If they were to ignore a temporary loss and stay invested, they could have been immersed in wealth instead. There is an old saying that "everything comes to you at the right moment. Be patient."

4. **Buying stocks randomly:** Don't go overboard with that buy button on your screen! I understand how addicting it can be, especially when you first get started. For instance, if you buy stocks from companies, you don't understand or fail to properly research and analyze, you will be throwing money out the window. When you understand the business, you know who they are and what their potential is. If you are big on technology and tech-savvy, you know the game and find those companies interesting. If you don't care about technology, why would you invest in tech businesses and research something which doesn't interest you? That doesn't make sense. Just because you transferred an amount to your online account doesn't mean you should burn through it buying random stocks just to get in the game, cheap or otherwise. Your purchase should be backed by solid research and growth potential, not just an adrenaline rush of excitement.

5. **Having super high expectations**: Don't expect too much or have high hopes. If you end up getting disappointed, it will put you in a rut. Yes, amazing things can happen in the stock market. Some people have turned $100 into $1000 and then into $10,000 or even a million! It is possible, but they did it with a clear and neutral head, following a strategy while managing their expectations. High hopes that you will gain a $1000 weekly profit straight off the bat is insane and almost impossible for beginners. Don't think you can do that at the start, especially with penny stocks. Most people play stocks as a lottery model and expect penny stocks to turn into thousands of dollars overnight.

   Even if you somehow achieve this much profit, it's absurd to move on with that attitude and mentality; it isn't sustainable. Realistic expectations never hurt; those that hurt you are unrealistic expectations and will only dishearten and demotivate you. Regardless, even if the numbers don't excite you that much right now, stick with it and trust in your research.

6. **Don't burn through your savings**: Undoubtedly, you have likely worked very hard for the money you have saved up. Trust me, I have been there, having had to support myself from a young age, working multiple jobs delivering pizzas, working in bars and restaurants, and saving every penny I could get my hands on. That took a lot of hard work! In stocks, if you rush and invest all your money right away, there is a fair chance that you might lose it all. Contemplate how you'd feel if you were to lose all of your hard-earned money. Invest some of it, not all of it. Invest it slowly, increasing your holdings over time. Your style, thinking, and risk tolerance decrease when you trade the only money you have. If you cannot afford to lose the

money, then don't invest it in the first place. Only invest what you can afford to lose—never forget this.

Are you willing to risk all your money today in the hope that you might gain a greater return tomorrow, despite understanding that you risk losing it all? If the answer to this is YES, genuinely, then only invest that amount of money, no more. Using the money you cannot afford to invest will overwhelm and pressure you into making stupid decisions and cause you to play with a cluttered, stressed mind. You want to be relaxed and calm at all times during an investment to make level-headed decisions.

7. **Not investing at all**: The final and most horrendous mistake you can ever make is not investing at all in the stock market. If you don't take action and invest, you may never live the life you always dreamed of. There are a variety of means to make money, but earning an income while you sleep is only gained through stocks and a handful of other investments. When you reach adulthood and eventually your retirement, life will be very expensive. It will cause you tremendous stress and anxiety if you are not financially sound. You will have considerable expenses to cover. A mortgage, food, clothes, and utilities. Responsibilities such as your own kids, their college educations, and living costs. Of course, inflation will be higher than it is now too. It can be terrifying to consider whether you will be able to afford it all. You don't want to be in a bad financial situation, nor do you want to only rely on one income source, such as a low-paid job. If you don't invest your money at all, there is no guarantee that you will manage it all; you do not want to be considered a failure in life, do you? The stock market is a sure source that will provide positive returns over the long run. Don't take unnecessary risks such as not acting at all. Instead,

take actionable risks that will reward you with freedom and abundance.

There you have it; the most common mistakes you could make if you were ignorant of the fact. Now that you know, the path is easier and much safer for you than before. Learn from each of these mistakes, and for those not listed here, you will learn through your own experience. One of the most effective learning methods, in my view, is through mistakes! Don't be afraid of short-term failures caused by making a mistake. When you take a fall, simply dust yourself off and get back on your feet. That's the beauty of the stock market; there are ups and downs but know that you can recover from them all. Let's recap what we learned in this chapter and then move on to the final step, where you will learn the biggest lesson of your life.

SUMMARY

1. It is only natural to get it wrong sometimes, and it's okay. Nobody learned anything from being perfect—nobody is perfect!

2. Be wise to learn from the mistakes listed herein to foresee and avoid them when the time comes. Here they are again:

   o Getting emotional

   o Following recommendations

   o Investing with a trader's mindset

   o Buying stocks randomly

   o Having super high expectations

   o Burning through your savings

   o Not investing at all

CHAPTER 8

STEP 7

LEARN FROM YOUR EXPERIENCE

"We do not learn from experience; we learn from reflecting on our experience."
— **John Dewey**

I ntroducing the final step in the process of making your dream a concrete reality. After you learn the lessons in this chapter, you will be ready to face the world of investing! Time and knowledge work in harmony while favoring and guiding you to the pinnacle that only a few people ever reach. It's called a place of abundance and freedom. In this place, you will be rich in all senses of the word. This chapter may be the final step in our journey in this book, but it is only the first step in yours.

You will grasp the importance of learning from your experiences, both good and bad. Be sure to incorporate the lessons you have learned into your future strategies to avoid common mistakes and ultimately improve positive outcomes. Scottish author, Samuel Smiles, said, *"The experience gathered from books, though often valuable, is but the nature of learning; whereas the experience gained from the actual life is one of the natures of wisdom."*

The future withholds unlimited opportunities for everyone; a few people seize them, and the majority just witness them from a distance. If life never stops giving you lemons, fetch some ice, salt, and sugar. It's time to enjoy the lemonade! That should be your attitude towards life and all the failures it has brought or is yet to bring in your life. Conversely, if you're presented with success, learn from the things that could have gone wrong and what you did that made you successful. While staying humble, learning from both situations is your ticket to the ranks of the ultra-wealthy. People like Richard Branson, Bill Gates, Elon Musk, Jeff Bezos, Warren Buffet, and other highly successful people. One day, you could be the proud owner of your own paradise island; you are only ever one trade away!

I've already told you, and I'll tell you again because you must digest these words and make it your second nature – BE PATIENT. I can't stress this enough. Be patient when it comes to the stock market. You will, at some point, experience sadness, anger, and no doubt, suffer losses, but it is only ever temporary. Because at some point, you will also experience happiness, excitement and make loads of profit. The reward of profit awaits on the other side of patience. Nobody gets rich overnight unless they win the lottery. Lionel Messi said, *"I start early and I stay late, day after day, year after year... It took me 17 years and 114 days to become an overnight success."* Most overnight successes result from years of hard work, dedication, perseverance, commitment, passion, and confidence. So, if you have any unrealistic ideas about becoming wealthy in a few weeks or months, get them out of your head—they will only serve to set unrealistic expectations, resulting in disappointment.

A SUCCESSFUL JOURNEY

Your strategy is something you stick to for years; it is your journey to success. Consistency is key. Much like going to the gym, results are only realized in the mid-long term. They are a result of strategic and consistent daily planning and action. When you are having a bad day and feel like giving up, remember why you started in the first place. Recall your purpose, the life you envisioned, the future you saw for yourself, and the people you want to help. This will get you through difficult situations, boredom, and failures. A person may achieve a million things in life, but there is almost always just one purpose behind them all. That's how powerful having a purpose is. It will teach you the skill of patience and harness the ability never to give up. Yes, following the same strategy you created over a long time might make you feel like there is no end to this, and you may get bored, though you need to stick with it to be successful! Celebrate every win along the way and keep yourself motivated. You have a higher chance of succeeding if you don't let your emotions get the best of you; remember chapter 7? Exactly! Don't make that mistake.

The first phase of your journey was educating yourself through reading this book and downloading the free investment resources on our website. The next is actually 'getting started,' one of the most challenging steps of them all. That phase will begin after you close this book. Treat your investment strategy as a journey to make it successful and prepare for the long term. Know that you are now an investor for a lifetime. No matter which business or industry you end up in later, you will always be an investor. So, plan your destination; determine what you want to achieve from investing in stocks. But, again, keep it realistic.

Your journey is an ever-changing one; you will need to educate yourself constantly, reading and learning as much as you can. It is impossible to stop learning; there will always be something you don't know or understand. Your job is to keep learning and apply that knowledge to the best of your abilities. Stay informed about what's going on in the markets. Attend those seminars, read those books, complete those courses, and listen to and learn from those who have crossed the finish line to success. You can develop simple rules that define your specific investment strategy—remember, set a goal, make a plan, and then execute it by following the process.

THE EXPERIENCE

The road to riches through the stock market is demanding but can also be thrilling and fun. As you experience the journey, note everything you are going through to learn from this experience later on. If you've made mistakes, mark them down. If you did something incredible that made you a significant profit or resulted in a win, mark it down. Focus on the highs and the lows and mark it down! The only way you can learn from your mistakes is if you have detailed data regarding the blunders and achievements. Keep a journal or record that showcases your complete journey. It's a very healthy habit to adopt. Keeping a journal will allow you to note down events and daily activities. Using timestamps, you can mention what you did on that particular date, and then you can also record your outcome. Furthermore, the companies you research can also go into your record after analyzing them and finally selecting them as a go-to investment. It is all part of your experience.

Another way to learn from experience is to ask people who have been where you are, that have traveled the same path. Maybe your parents, a relative, or a friend who has investment experience. Learning from others is an essential weapon to have in your arsenal. Seek guidance when you need to. The best way to learn as part of your advanced learning curve is through an experienced mentor who is ahead of the game so that you can walk the same path to success. This person can help you prevent the mistakes they made. It is an excellent way to learn something without going through the trauma of loss and regret. Not only will you get an indication of any pitfalls, but you will also get the solution to the problem prior to its occurrence. People love sharing their stories and successes. A mentor will gladly tell you how they defeated tough times, market crashes, and what it took for them to prevail despite the odds.

Stock Market Investing is a trial-and-error process, and you need to have the will to learn. The market is very unpredictable, but your control over your own strategy can achieve incredible things.

When you monitor your progress, you can evaluate your performance and readjust accordingly to get back on track if you find something off-putting. This, when followed consistently, will cultivate the good habit of learning from your own experience. Identify other high-achieving investors, and you will find that they stick with the good habits that make them more money. If you start early on in your teen years, you could be financially free by the age of 21 if you choose to be. If you have not developed good habits yet, don't worry, it's never too late. Get up early, take care of your health, get a job so you can save as much as you can to reinvest, learn to reflect on your past, keep learning, and help those people in need. These are some excellent principles to live by. Those are some great habits to have in life in general. So, why don't you start with them? Lewis Howes said, *"I've learned that champions aren't just born; champions can be made when they embrace and commit to life-changing positive habits."*

Similarly, if you can build new habits, you can also banish some of the bad habits you may be used to. When you reflect, you will notice that your mistakes were likely due to a particular personality trait; your habits can make you do negative things. When you can pinpoint what that bad habit is, you should try to get rid of it. Benjamin Franklin said, *"It is easier to prevent bad habits than to break them."*

There is one more thing without which nothing is worth doing—the ability to be consistent about it. No matter how great your strategy, how awesome your goal, how excited you are, and how powerful the support from other people is, you will eventually fail if you do not remain consistent. They always say that consistency is key. No success in the whole world was ever achieved without consistent application.

Let's review what we learned, and then we can move on to the key takeaways.

SUMMARY

1. It is essential to learn from your good and bad experiences and incorporate these lessons into your future to avoid mistakes and improve positive outcomes.

2. Be Patient. I can't stress this enough. When it comes to achieving your stock market successes, patience is key.

3. Most overnight successes result from years of hard work, dedication, passion, commitment, and confidence. Unfortunately, apart from winning the lottery, there are very few actual overnight successes in reality.

4. You shouldn't get bored of sticking to the same plan over the long term.

5. Having a purpose will teach you the skill of patience and harness the ability never to give up—that's how powerful it is.

6. Getting started is one of the most challenging yet most rewarding steps.

7. Treat your investing phase as a journey. To make it successful, prepare for the long term.

8. Learning is a lifelong activity; there will always be something you don't know. Your job is to be a sponge and learn as much as possible, applying them to the best of your abilities.

9. Keep a journal, make a note of everything you're going through, the positive as well as the negative. It will help you make a detailed analysis of your performance later in the journey.

10. Learning from others is an important tool you have in your arsenal. So, don't be ashamed or afraid to seek guidance when you need it.

11. Find a mentor and learn from them. Don't ever forget that I am here to help guide you along the way.

12. The market is very unpredictable, but your control over your own strategy can achieve incredible things.

13. Monitor your own progress, evaluate your performance, and readjust accordingly.

14. Cultivate good habits and banish the bad ones.

15. Be consistent on your journey.

CONCLUSION

KEY TAKEAWAYS

"Take action! An inch of movement will bring you closer to your goals than a mile of intention."
– Steve Maraboli

Most people start a journey but don't make it till the end; don't be that person. You have proven that you really care about your future, and you're determined to achieve your purpose. I am thrilled to know that. We started with the goal of empowering you to invest so that when you reach your twenties, you will already have a well-established path to financial freedom. If you consistently follow this simple guide with its 7-step system, you will have a solid foundation. You grasped those stocks are the most important option in your investment portfolio. There is no other investment that offers the same benefits and profits over the long run.

Investing in stocks could be tricky, and the stock market is unpredictable; that said, you can still invest and make a handsome profit from it. Do not fall victim to peer pressure. Invest only in the things you understand. Stocks defy the effect of inflation and taxes, and when you hold a stock for a long time, you are building yourself a future. Time is in your favor as a teen because, presumably, you have the most time to learn and make mistakes. Also, you can hold your stocks for a more extended period. Do not get discouraged by the myths; move past this.

In summary, let's recap what we discussed in the book step by step. Are you with me? Let's begin!

Step 1: SPEAK THE LANGUAGE OF STOCKS

To attain a deep and meaningful relationship with the stock market, you must learn to speak the same language. To learn the language, all you need to do is understand the terms used and learn them thoroughly, their meaning, and when to use them. Then, insert them into your vocabulary, and you will be on par with the professionals.

Step 2: GETTING INTO THE GAME

The first step is usually the most difficult to take, but once you do, you will be glad you did because countless opportunities await you when you start playing the game of stocks. To get into the game, you will need to:

- Open your bank account.

- Choose the type of investment account you want. There are three types: Standard Brokerage Account, Investment Account for Kids, and a Retirement Account.

- Select an online trader to begin your journey. Choose your online broker wisely; the list includes Charles Schwab, Stockpile, Ally Invest, E-Trade, TD Ameritrade, Loved Investing, and Fidelity. Of course, there are more, but these are my favorites.

- If you haven't already, be sure to check out www.jp-clarke.com/resources, where I have put together some very useful resources, including links to various websites & brokerages, budgeting & goal-setting tools, free downloads, and other handy information to help get you started on your investment journey.

Step 3: WRAPPING YOUR HEAD AROUND THE BASICS

The stock market is where investors and companies unite to buy and sell shares in the public domain – NYSE and Nasdaq are where the magic happens. Investing in stocks is easy. The general rule of thumb is, buy a stock when it is low, wait until it increases in value, then sell the stock for a profit. To keep track of all the stocks and their performance, you need a market platform; it could be an online website, software, or an application.

Stocks are distributed in four categories, Individual Shares, Fractional Shares, Exchange Trading Funds or ETFs, and Index Funds. Someone sells the stock, and the other buys it. Buyers and sellers negotiate the price of a stock; hence, trade is made. Once you know what you want to invest in, you need a specific strategy to stick to for the long term. For maximum profit, trade both individual stocks and index funds.

Step 4: DECIDING YOUR INVESTMENTS

When it comes to selecting the best stocks to buy, there are two strategies you will use in conducting your research:

1. Qualitative Analysis (non-numbers based), and

2. Quantitative Analysis (numbers based)

Qualitative Analysis focuses on non-numbers-based data such as what the company does and how it makes its money, who runs it, its growth potential, and its competitive advantage.

Quantitative Analysis focuses on the facts and numbers; this is where we will look at the company's financials in detail to see how it is performing.

Find great stocks using Qualitative Analysis by:

- Looking where you spend your money already.

- Investing in companies you understand.

- Looking at growing industries.

- Finding the companies with strong leadership.

- Finding companies that have competitive advantages.

Find great stocks using Quantitative Analysis by:

- Checking the chart to see the share price trend showing a steady increase over the long term.

- Check its market cap to understand the size of the company.

- Check the P/E ratio to identify if the company is profitable or not. Remember, if there is a number, it is profitable, and if there is no number or shows N/A, then it isn't.

- Check if the company has more cash than debt by using the market cap and enterprise values. If the market cap figure is higher than the enterprise value, the company has more cash than debt and vice versa.

- Check that the annual financials for each year/period show an increase in Total Revenue and Gross Profits year on year.

- Check the company's Gross Margin % on Morningstar.com; ideally, we want to see $\geq$ 30%.

- Check that the Net Income AND Total Revenue increase simultaneously.

- Check what the analysts are saying regarding Revenue and Earnings estimates growth.

- Determine the fair value of the stock by dividing the market cap by the number of shares available. If the current share price is lesser than fair value, it could be an excellent time to buy.

- Make an excel sheet to record your research.

- When deciding when to buy, if the share price is going down, find the bottom price by waiting for it to go down and then buy as soon as you see it starting to increase.

Step 5: STRATEGIZE AND ORGANIZE

Decide on a concrete result or outcome that you want to achieve which satisfies and makes you happy. Then, create a definitive strategy using specific and measurable goals to achieve that result. No goal can be achieved without the creation of a concise, actionable plan. Choose the one that will take you towards your purpose quickly and with fewer risks. There are many benefits of having a strategy like being proactive, less procrastination, an efficient and optimized path, and a clear sense of direction. Here are a few strategies to get you started:

- Growth Investing
- Value Investing
- Diversification

Step 6: DODGING THE MISTAKES

You're going to make a lot of errors, and it's okay. Make as many as you can and learn from them, do not repeat the same mistake twice. Here are a few errors that you can avoid:

- Getting emotional
- Following recommendations

- Investing with a trader's mindset

- Buying stocks randomly

- Having super high expectations

- Burning through your savings

- Not investing at all

Step 7: LEARN FROM YOUR EXPERIENCE

It is essential to learn from your experience, both good and bad, and incorporate the lessons you learned into the future to avoid mistakes and improve positive outcomes. For this to work, you should first learn and understand one of the most required skills of an investor—being patient. Overnight success is a myth. Most overnight successes result from years of hard work, dedication, perseverance, commitment, passion, and confidence. Build a strategy and stick to it for the long term. Do not get bored. Prepare yourself for a long journey, and always keep learning. Track your progress with a journal. Mark all your events, profits, loss, and the things you learned.

It doesn't matter if you gain a quick profit or lose a few pennies; the critical part is that you keep going regardless. Learn from yourself and others, get a mentor who can narrate their story to you. Feel free to reach out to me for guidance. Monitor your progress; you can evaluate your performance and readjust accordingly. To gain profit, you should be able to cultivate some good habits within you, and at the same time, banish the ones that are causing harm to your financial success.

I have taken great pleasure in teaching you the 7 Steps to Financial Independence on the Stock Market. You must apply the knowledge, principles, and laws in real life and begin your journey as an investor. Your future self will be massively benefitted as a result. I am so excited to see you grow and become wealthy. I wish I could hear about your story and how this book impacted and helped you. That said, there is a way that you can share your experience with me and many others who would benefit from this journey. Please submit a review on Amazon if you appreciate this book. I can't wait to read your comments!

Get support from other like-minded investors and me by scanning the QR code shown below. You will find links to all the below resources or visit www.jp-clarke.com. Make sure you:

1. Like my **Facebook page**

2. Join other investors and me in our **Facebook Group**

3. **Download your free investment resources** valued at **$149.00!**

4. Check out the free resources page for loads of useful tools, links, and downloads

5. Check out my other books **on Amazon**

https://qrco.de/bcHRo3

Reach out to me at jp@jp-clarke.com should you need any assistance or have any questions at all. Every step of the way, I'll be there for you! Until then, keep learning and keep investing...

Want to receive all my future books for FREE before they are released to the public?

Visit jp-clarke.com/reviewteam to find out more.

$149

FREE

**INVESTING CHEATSHEET
TOP 3 STOCKS TO BUY NOW
110 PASSIVE INCOME IDEAS
COMPANY RESEARCH STRATEGY**

RESOURCES

7 Steps to a Successful Investment Journey. (n.d.). Investopedia. Retrieved June 1, 2021, from
https://www.investopedia.com/investing/steps-successful-investment-journey/
Avoid These 8 Common Investing Mistakes. (n.d.). Investopedia. Retrieved June 1, 2021, from
https://www.investopedia.com/articles/stocks/07/beat_the_mistakes.asp#3-lack-of-patience
Be Patient With Me Quotes. QuotesGram. (n.d.). Quotesgram. Retrieved June 1, 2021, from
https://quotesgram.com/be-patient-with-me-quotes/
Bertrand Russell Quote. (n.d.). A-Z Quotes. Retrieved June 1, 2021, from
https://www.azquotes.com/quote/254938
A Breakdown on How the Stock Market Works. (n.d.). Investopedia. Retrieved June 1, 2021, from
https://www.investopedia.com/articles/investing/082614/how-stock-market-works.asp
Burks, R. (2014, December 15). *High School Student Becomes A Stock Market Millionaire During His
Lunch Break*. Tech Times. https://www.techtimes.com/articles/22224/20141215/high-school-student-
becomes-a-stock-market-multimillionaire.htm
Business Insider India. (n.d.). *THE 20 UNDER 20: Meet The Teen Traders Who Plan To Take Over
The World Of Finance*. Business Insider. Retrieved June 1, 2021, from
https://www.businessinsider.in/finance/the-20-under-20-meet-the-teen-traders-who-plan-to-take-over-
the-world-of-finance/slidelist/25453482.cms#slideid=25588021
Common Investing Mistakes You Need to Avoid. (n.d.). The Balance. Retrieved June 1, 2021, from
https://www.thebalance.com/common-investing-mistakes-you-must-avoid-4104189
Corporate Finance Institute. (2020, January 7). *Growth Stocks*.
https://corporatefinanceinstitute.com/resources/knowledge/trading-investing/growth-
stocks/#:%7E:text=Apple%20Inc.,very%20brand%20loyal%20consumer%20base.
Correspondent, H. T. (2020, November 19). *Kanishk Gupta is one of the youngest entrepreneurs in
Indian stock market*. Hindustan Times. https://www.hindustantimes.com/brand-post/kanishk-gupta-is-
one-of-the-youngest-entrepreneurs-in-indian-stock-market/story-UAnfUejVx5FHVew8T18CiI.html
How to Invest as a Teenager or a Minor. (n.d.). TeenVestor. Retrieved June 1, 2021, from
https://www.teenvestor.com/7steps
Investment Strategies To Learn Before Trading. (n.d.). Investopedia. Retrieved June 1, 2021, from
https://www.investopedia.com/investing/investing-strategies/
Iz quotes wisdom Pin on quotes. (n.d.). Dogtrainingobedienceschool. Retrieved June 1, 2021, from
https://dogtrainingobedienceschool.com/iz-quotes-wisdom/4404670_pin-on-quotes.html
Joyce Meyer Quotes. (n.d.). BrainyQuote. Retrieved June 1, 2021, from
https://www.brainyquote.com/quotes/joyce_meyer_567645
K. (2019, April 24). *Value Investing Quotes, Sayings, & Proverbs: Wisest Men Compilation*. Arbor
Asset Allocation Model Portfolio (AAAMP) Value Blog.
https://www.arborinvestmentplanner.com/wisest-value-investing-quotes-sayings-money-proverbs/
Kapoor, N. (2019, September 5). *5 most successful young investors*. YourStory.Com.
https://yourstory.com/mystory/809961765f-5-most-successful-youn/amp
Krishna, R. (2020, May 22). *5 Common Stock Investing Mistakes to Avoid as a Beginner*. Groww.
https://groww.in/blog/common-stock-investing-mistakes-to-avoid-as-a-beginner/
Lagacé, M. (2021, March 13). *115 Mistakes Quotes That Will Make You Braver*. Wisdom Quotes.
https://wisdomquotes.com/mistakes-quotes/
Mark Cuban Quote: âIf you donât follow the stock market, you are missing some amazing drama.â.
(n.d.). Quote Fancy. Retrieved June 1, 2021, from https://quotefancy.com/quote/1151982/Mark-
Cuban-If-you-don-t-follow-the-stock-market-you-are-missing-some-amazing-drama

Meah, A. (2019, May 4). *35 Inspirational Quotes On Strategy*. AwakenTheGreatnessWithin.
https://www.awakenthegreatnesswithin.com/35-inspirational-quotes-on-strategy/
Mercadante, K. (n.d.). *5 Golden Rules for Choosing the Best Stock*. Doughroller.
https://www.doughroller.net/investing/5-golden-rules-for-choosing-the-best-stock/
Nguyen, H. (2021, January 16). *7 Biggest Benefits and Drawbacks of Value Investing | Wealthy Education - Investing Strategies That Work!* Wealthy Education.
https://wealthyeducation.com/benefits-and-drawbacks-of-value-investing/?doing_wp_cron=1621953693.6268129348754882812500
Online, F. E. (2019, September 30). *Explained: Why it is necessary to keep your emotions in check while investing*. The Financial Express. https://www.financialexpress.com/money/explained-why-it-is-necessary-to-keep-your-emotions-in-check-while-investing/1722541/
O'Shea, A. (2021a, April 26). *Stock Market Basics: What Beginner Investors Should Know*. NerdWallet. https://www.nerdwallet.com/article/investing/stock-market-basics-everything-beginner-investors-know
O'Shea, A. (2021b, May 3). *What Is the Stock Market and How Does It Work?* NerdWallet. https://www.nerdwallet.com/article/investing/what-is-the-stock-market
Peter Lynch quote. (n.d.-a). QuoteNova.Net. Retrieved June 1, 2021, from https://www.quotenova.net/authors/peter-lynch/qapgzv
Peter Lynch Quote. (n.d.-b). A-Z Quotes. Retrieved June 1, 2021, from https://www.azquotes.com/quote/181350
Peter Lynch Quote. (n.d.-c). A-Z Quotes. Retrieved June 1, 2021, from https://www.azquotes.com/quote/814612
Q. (n.d.-a). *Investment quotes, Investing, Einstein*. Pinterest. Retrieved June 1, 2021, from https://www.pinterest.com/pin/investing-in-the-stock-market--820710732067295720/
Q. (n.d.-b). *Master Your Emotions | Awareness quotes, Emotion words, Judgement quotes*. Pinterest. Retrieved June 1, 2021, from https://www.pinterest.com/pin/288863763600389058/
Quotes, S. (2020, February 25). *75 Quotes that Prove Overnight Success is a Myth*. SHINE QUOTES. https://shinequotes.com/overnight-success-quotes/
Say, J. (2020, June 27). *52 Philip Fisher Quotes (LEGENDARY INVESTOR)*. Gracious Quotes. https://graciousquotes.com/philip-fisher/
Singh, N. (2020, December 5). *5 Youngest Successful Stock Traders in the World*. TradeVeda. https://tradeveda.com/youngest-stock-traders/#:%7E:text=Brandon%20Fleisher%20is%20a%2022,still%20a%20high%20school%20senior.
Singh, P. (2020, February 5). *Quote on Long-term Goals by Charles C. Noble*. Dont Give Up World. https://dontgiveupworld.com/quote-on-long-term-goals-by-charles-c-noble/
Staff, S. (2018, July 31). *17 Motivational Quotes to Inspire Successful Habits*. SUCCESS. https://www.success.com/17-motivational-quotes-to-inspire-successful-habits/
Stock Investment Strategies. (n.d.). TeenVestor. Retrieved June 1, 2021, from https://www.teenvestor.com/stock-investment-strategies
Stock Market Quotes To Make You A Better Investor. (2020, October 22). YourSelf Quotes. https://www.yourselfquotes.com/stock-market-quotes/
Things never work out quotes But things work out you know even if it doesnt feel okay for a. (n.d.). Dog Training Obedience School. Retrieved June 1, 2021, from https://dogtrainingobedienceschool.com/things-never-work-out-quotes/6187576_but-things-work-out-you-know-even-if-it-doesnt-feel-okay-for-a.html
Thomas Edison quotes - I have not failed. I've just found 10,000 ways that won't work. (2017, May 31). Goalcast. https://www.goalcast.com/2017/05/11/thomas-edison-quotes-motivate-never-quit/thomas-edison-quotes-i-have-not-failed-ive-just-found-10000-ways-that-wont-work/
TOP 25 LEARNING EXPERIENCE QUOTES (of 164). (n.d.). A-Z Quotes. Retrieved June 1, 2021, from https://www.azquotes.com/quotes/topics/learning-experience.html
TradingStrategyGuides. (2020, October 29). *Top Trading Quotes of All Time*. https://tradingstrategyguides.com/top-trading-quotes-of-all-time-learn-to-trade/
Warren Buffett Quote: âWe don't have to be smarter than the rest. We have to be more disciplined than the rest.â. (n.d.). Quote Fancy. Retrieved June 1, 2021, from https://quotefancy.com/quote/931002/Warren-Buffett-We-don-t-have-to-be-smarter-than-the-rest-We-have-to-be-more-disciplined
We are what we repeatedly do. Excellence, then, is not an act but a habit. - Will Durant | Focus quotes, Inspirational quotes, Genius quotes. (n.d.). Pinterest. Retrieved June 1, 2021, from https://www.pinterest.com/pin/648448046337687711/

Wei, J. (2021, February 23). *Robert Arnott – What is Comfortable is Rarely Profitable*. Due.
https://due.com/blog/robert-arnott-what-is-comfortable-is-rarely-profitable/
When you make a #mistake, there are only three things you should ever do about it: admit it, #learn from it, and don't repeat it. | Mistake quotes, Words quotes, Meaningful quotes. (n.d.). Pinterest.
Retrieved June 1, 2021, from https://www.pinterest.co.uk/pin/when-you-make-a-mistake-there-are-only-three-things-you-should-ever-do-about-it-admit-it-learn-from-it-and-dont-repeat-it--55380270398807079/
Wikipedia contributors. (2021, April 24). *Lifelong learning*. Wikipedia.
https://en.wikipedia.org/wiki/Lifelong_learning
Yochim, D. (2021a, March 17). *4 Types of Investment Accounts You Should Know*. NerdWallet.
https://www.nerdwallet.com/article/investing/types-investment-accounts-know
Yochim, D. (2021b, May 25). *How to Research Stocks*. NerdWallet.
https://www.nerdwallet.com/article/investing/how-to-research-stocks
$tock 101. (n.d.). The Truth Success Series. Retrieved 21 September 2021, from https://christons-school.thinkific.com/courses/tock-101
Brett Sifling | Investment Advisor Representative | Gerber Wealth. (n.d.). Brett Sifling. Retrieved 21 September 2021, from https://gerberkawasaki.com/team/brett-sifling Chakraborty, A. (2019, November 3). Circle of Competence: How Warren Buffett Avoids Failures. Abhishek Chakraborty.
https://coffeeandjunk.com/circle-of-competence/
Cliff, M. (2021, February 24). Teen shares how he turned £200 into £200k in year after learning about shares on YouTube. . . The Sun. https://www.thesun.co.uk/fabulous/14142017/teen-makes-200k-one-year-stock-market/
Ed Seykota Quote. (n.d.). A-Z Quotes. Retrieved 21 September 2021, from
https://www.azquotes.com/quote/800903
Figure Out Your Investment Goals. (n.d.). Investopedia. Retrieved 21 September 2021, from
https://www.investopedia.com/investing/figure-out-your-investment-goals/
Gillespie, P. (2015, March 4). The millennial investor raking in a 250% return. CNNMoney.
https://money.cnn.com/2015/03/04/investing/how-to-invest-millennial-justin-brosseau/?iid=EL
How To Pick Great Stocks | Step By Step Qualitative Analysis. (2021, February 28). YouTube.
https://www.youtube.com/watch?v=3dy1IgZOrwA&pp=sAQA
Kollmeyer, B. (2021a, March 13). How these teens are having fun in today's stock market, and, for the most part, making money. MarketWatch. https://www.marketwatch.com/story/these-teens-are-having-fun-in-todays-stock-market-they-share-the-secrets-to-their-success-11615218810
Kollmeyer, B. (2021b, March 15). A new wave of fearless retail investors is ready to pour $170 billion into stocks, predicts Deutsche Bank. MarketWatch. https://www.marketwatch.com/story/a-new-wave-of-fearless-retail-investors-could-be-ready-to-pour-170-billion-into-stocks-says-deutsche-bank-11614253899
Post Page. (n.d.). The Urban Metro Gator Site. Retrieved 21 September 2021, from
https://theurbanmetro.gator.site/home/christon-truth-jones-the-teenage-stock-market-prodigy
Step By Step Quantitative Analysis | Stock Analysis for Beginners. (2021, March 9). YouTube.
https://www.youtube.com/watch?v=YEGkVUnbLso&t=5s&pp=sAQA
Taylor, M. E. (2019, February 14). How this 11-year-old day trader fought bullies to make $10,000 on the stock market. Face2Face Africa. https://face2faceafrica.com/article/how-this-11-year-old-day-trader-fought-bullies-to-make-10000-on-the-stock-market
Top 6 Reasons New Businesses Fail. (n.d.). Investopedia. Retrieved 21 September 2021, from
https://www.investopedia.com/financial-edge/1010/top-6-reasons-new-businesses-fail.aspx#:%7E:text=According%20to%20the%20U.S.%20Bureau,to%2015%20years%20or%20more
The Top 25 Investing Quotes of All Time. (n.d.). Investopedia. Retrieved 21 September 2021, from
https://www.investopedia.com/financial-edge/0511/the-top-17-investing-quotes-of-all-time.aspx
Kraakman, N. (n.d.). Lessons from Rich Dad, Poor Dad (summary). Robert Kiyosaki | Value Investing Blog by Nick Kraakman. Retrieved 17 November 2021, from
https://www.valuespreadsheet.com/blog/rich-dad-poor-dad-summary-robert-kiyosaki
Balogun, T. (2019, March 20). How Christon Jones, 11-year-old Day Trader Fought Bullies to Make $10,000 on the Stock Market. Espact. Retrieved 25 November 2021, from https://espact.com/how-christon-jones-11-year-old-day-trader-fought-bullies-to-make-10000-on-the-stock-market/

Made in the USA
Middletown, DE
18 April 2022

64188335R00084